EPIC
MARKETPLACE
REVIVAL

DOING BUSINESS
GOD'S WAY

WALT KALLESTAD
WITH BLAKNEY KALLESTAD

MEDIA.COM

Epic Marketplace Revival

Copyright © 2025 by Walt and Blakney Kallestad

Published by
Illumify Media Global
www.IllumifyMedia.com
"Let's bring your book to life!"

Unless otherwise indicated, all Scripture quotations are from The Passion Translation®. Copyright © 2017, 2018, 2020 by Passion & Fire Ministries, Inc. Used by permission. All rights reserved. ThePassionTranslation.com.

Scripture quotations marked (NKJV) are taken from New King James Version®. Copyright © 1982 by Thomas Nelson. Used by permission. All rights reserved.

Scripture quotations marked (NLT) are taken from *Holy Bible*, New Living Translation, copyright © 1996, 2004, 2015 by Tyndale House Foundation. Used by permission of Tyndale House Publishers, Inc., Carol Stream, Illinois 60188. All rights reserved.

Scripture quotations marked (NIV) are taken from The Holy Bible, New International Version® NIV® Copyright © 1973, 1978, 1984, 2011 by Biblica, Inc.® Used by Permission of Biblica, Inc.® All rights reserved worldwide.

Library of Congress Control Number: 2025913074

Paperback ISBN: 978-1-964251-72-1
Hardcover ISBN: 978-1-964251-73-8

Cover design by Debbie Lewis

Printed in the United States of America

ENDORSEMENTS

"My friend Walt Kallestad has inspired and encouraged millions around the world to lead like Jesus led and live like Jesus lived as well as love as Jesus loved. I enthusiastically endorse Walt's twentieth book for everyone who desires to be a part of a global movement to 'Do Business God's Way!' I wholeheartedly believe that everyone should read *Epic Marketplace Revival*, no matter what stage of business or life you are in!"

John Maxwell, globally known business-leadership speaker, author of ninety-four books with sales of thirty-nine million copies, including New York Times bestseller *The 21 Irrefutable Laws of Leadership*

"*Epic Marketplace Revival: Doing Business God's Way* is a must-read for anyone who is committed to investing their time, talent, and treasure in areas that will bring everlasting significance and value, not simply temporary worth. My friend Walt Kallestad has committed his entire life to 'all things eternal.' Read this book and be part of the Epic Marketplace Revival!"

Ken Blanchard, author of *The One Minute Manager* and *Servant Leadership in Action*

"I thank God for my friend Walt Kallestad, who has dedicated his life to encouraging everyone wherever he goes to be a Marketplace Soul-Winner. Walt has been an encouragement for me to use all my success in sports and in business to build my Heavenly Father's Kingdom and not my own."

Jerry Colangelo, former owner of NBA Phoenix Suns and MLB Diamondbacks

"This book reveals how to seamlessly unite our Christian faith with our business pursuits, breaking down boundaries so God can open doors to a truly impactful career—one that thrives without compromising our faith."

Rickey M. "Rick" Warner, Senior Vice President, CBRE/Advisory & Transaction Services

"This is a must-read for anyone ready to align their professional purpose with their divine calling. Walt's book is a profound reminder that our talents and mission are ultimately meant to build the Kingdom of God. *Epic Marketplace Revival: Doing Business God's Way* is for those who want to hear the words, 'well done, my good and faithful servant' at the end of their lives, while letting God prosper the work of their hands in the here and now. Walt has written a Holy Spirit Masterpiece that will touch your heart."

Dino Prato, Founder & CEO, Envita Medical Centers

"As an entrepreneur and business owner, I am humbled and honored to wholeheartedly endorse the amazing book, *Epic Marketplace Revival: Doing Business God's Way*. This book inspires me to continue walking out God's call on my life to pastor and move in the marketplace one cookie at a time where we are determined to build the Kingdom and see people set free. My business has always been modeled on the same Biblical principles that Walt and Blakney have so excellently written about in this book. I highly recommend that every businessperson seeking true godly success dive into reading this book; keeping in mind it's not about the bottom line but saving souls and setting people free."

Verlie Payne, pastry chef, entrepreneur, and founder of Hudson's Cookies

"Ezra Pound once said: 'It's not for lack of writing ability that there are not more great writers, it's for lack of character.' Precisely that godly character of Dr. Kallestad has enabled him to capture 'The Way' for success in the marketplace. Twenty-five years ago, he appealed to me to put into practice what *Epic Marketplace Revival* details—into an Internal Medicine practice. It's been so transformative that the staff insists we carve out 'hands together' prayer time no matter how busy the day surrounding us. The years of practicing this have delivered their families into generational prosperity—and out of darkness."

Frank Agnone, **M.D.**, Internal Medicine, Phoenix, Arizona

"My dear friend Walt has done it again! His book, *Epic Marketplace Revival: Doing Business God's Way* is laser focused on living life with our eternal bottom line—the measure of all we do. In the book, he casts a vision that is both challenging and encouraging at the same time and motivates the reader to prioritize the great issues of life in sync with God's plan for our lives. The book is a great tool to help live life with eternal significance."

Bob Belz, author, teacher, pastor, and film and television producer and consultant. Bob was part of the producing team on *The Bible Series* on the *History Channel*, the Chronicles of Narnia films, and *Amazing Grace*, among others.

"As a young entrepreneur in my early 30's, I've leaned on personal development books and resources to help me carve out a path to success. But what I've mostly found is a sea of white noise—'gurus' feeding my generation click-bait, vanity metrics, and shallow definitions of success. *Epic Marketplace Revival: Doing Business God's Way* cuts through that noise, offering a blueprint to business rooted in scripture, backed by the fruit of a life devoted to building God's Kingdom in the marketplace. Walt's story isn't just inspiring—it's a charge for every entrepreneur to make God's business our business, to let our work shine as a light in the marketplace, and to use our gifts to win souls for eternity."

Esther Cottle, Author & Co-Founder of The Christian Entrepreneur Club

"The greatest move of God we've ever seen is happening right now through Christian business leaders in the marketplace. *Epic Marketplace Revival: Doing Business God's Way* is a book written at a revolutionary time to equip Christians to build businesses with God and for God. This is a must read for those of us that feel called to build businesses and advance God's Kingdom. Walt and Blakney thank you for passing on your wisdom to the next generation to carry the torch and bring revival to the marketplace."

Cody Cottle, Co-Founder and President of
The Christian Entrepreneur Club

DEDICATION

We would like to dedicate this book to the greatest, richest, wisest, humblest, friendliest, most giving, most forgiving, mightiest, and most trustworthy person who has ever lived and the only one who has ever died and rose again for everyone who has ever walked and will ever walk the face of the Earth—His name is JESUS.

REVIVAL

<u>R</u>EPENTANCE

<u>E</u>VERLASTING

<u>V</u>ICTORIOUS

<u>I</u>GNITING

<u>V</u>IBRANT

<u>A</u>LL-IN

<u>L</u>IFE-GIVING

—Walt Kallestad

CONTENTS

PREFACE

Have you ever wrestled with God? I have. Many times. And I struggled when God's desires and plans for my life were not aligned with my own plans and sense of purpose. I am reminded of God's story of Jacob's wrestling match with Him. Jacob relentlessly wrestled with God to give him a blessing that would enable Jacob to live his life doing what he wanted to do! Yet in wrestling with God, Jacob ended up with a different but massive blessing, including a new name. His original name, Jacob, meant "heel grabber," and when God changed it to Israel, it meant "one who struggled with God and prevailed."[1]

Even though Jacob ended up with a limp that came from a torn hip socket while wrestling with God, Jacob's, now Israel's, perseverance ended up being so blessed by God that it propelled Israel's life to succeed and prosper beyond his greatest dreams or imagination.

During my senior year of college, one of the deepest struggles I brought before God was whether to become an ordained pastor. I remember telling God, I was never going to be a youth director, pastor, or ever work in a church!

This stance was rooted in watching my mom and dad pastor churches where some of the members said things that were extremely hurtful and unkind. One time in particular, my parents sat sobbing at our kitchen table. In that moment I found myself crying out to God once again and telling Him I never wanted to be a pastor or work in a church. It always amazes me how God will allow us to claim "never" for a season, but then He will soften our hearts to the very thing we told God "no" to.

Well—I ended up as a youth director in Burnsville, Minnesota, and in 1978, following seminary graduation, I became an ordained pastor at the same church. Following my ordination as a pastor, God sent me to Arizona, where I pastored one church for over forty years. As you can see, God won our wrestling match, as He always does!

My most recent wrestling match with God was in writing this book. I told God I was done authoring. But God made it clear to me that He has big plans for businesses who want to say YES and commit to doing business God's way. My heart burned continuously to be a part of igniting a marketplace revival. My heart just will not say no to God. As usual, God won and allowed me to answer His call to share the joy of doing business God's way through this book.

Doing business God's way creates an amazing platform to share the Gospel of Jesus with millions of people. Being a light in the business world means introducing people from all walks of life to Jesus and inviting them to wholeheartedly and enthusiastically come to love, follow, serve, please, and enjoy Him forever! I assure you that I am honored to have been chosen as an instrument to author this book. My wife Blakney and I pray that together we will globally be able to partner with all who join in this Epic Marketplace Revival movement to Do Business God's Way.

ACKNOWLEDGMENTS

Following my late wife Mary's journey to Heaven, God blessed me with an amazing, godly woman who is a true treasure to me from God. I want to honor and thank my beloved wife Blakney for encouraging, cowriting, and praying for and with me throughout this past year of authoring *Epic Marketplace Revival*.

I also want to enthusiastically thank my marketplace friends for their wisdom, encouragement and endorsements. These friends are truly God-honoring Epic Marketplace Revivalists.

—Walt Kallestad

What a privilege to cowrite this book with my amazing husband, Walt. I never thought I would be a pastor's wife, but God knew. God prepared my heart to seek after Him all the days of my life. So, when God placed the most amazing man in my life to be my husband, it was an immediate and resounding YES. I cannot imagine pursuing after God with anyone other than Walt. Walt's unwavering love and support to the covenant marriage we have is truly one of a kind. (Stay tuned for our next book about doing marriage God's way. It's a God-tale, you will not want to miss!)

I also want to thank my sweet mother, who prayed with unwavering love for a godly husband for me. God blessed me with an angel when God gave her to me as my mom.

—Blakney Kallestad

As our hearts overflow with gratitude, we want to thank and acknowledge our Illumify Media team, our treasured friend Victor Currie for his direction with media, and Rebekah Barlow for tirelessly taking Walt's handwritten scribbling and putting it into legible form.

We are grateful God gave us an amazing prayer team this last year, including the Mighty Oaks (Frank Agnone, Bjorn Pedersen, Don "Doon" Crawley), Susan Wells, Larry and Staci Wallace, Irina Ilie, Geoff and Suzanne Ewertz, Cathy Marshall, Diana Warner, Dena Stitt, Allen and Julie Anjo, Lynn Newell, and Towmika Young. Prayer moves mountains!

INTRODUCTION

This book has been written with a burning passion to ignite an unstoppable marketplace revival, one that will demonstrate overwhelming evidence of the transformational power of Jesus Christ by changing your business from a profit-driven endeavor to a soul-winning-driven mission. Profits are always temporary. People transformed through the unlimited grace and unconditional love of Jesus Christ is always permanent.

Every word of *Epic Marketplace Revival: Doing Business God's Way* has been accompanied with unceasing prayer. As I prayed and studied what the Bible says about how to run a business that is destined for eternal success, I was amazed how doing business God's way is not only the best way to run a successful business—it's the *only* way to guarantee a successful business that will last for an eternity.

This book has many direct quotes from the Bible because I believe what God says will assure eternal success. The Bible is God's manual for operating our lives, which includes our businesses. If I only used my words, I would be doing you a disservice. While what I have to say may be helpful, God's words are what supernaturally change lives and offer everlasting wisdom and understanding about how to truly succeed God's way.

Think about how incredibly powerful God's words are to cause miracles to happen. God's words raise the dead, heal the sick, bring sight to the blind, make the deaf hear again, and much more. God's words give eternal life in Heaven to everyone who repents and believes in Jesus, the Savior of the World.

The following men and women are examples of great champions for Christ in the marketplace: Barbara and David Greene, the founders of Hobby Lobby; Truitt Cathy of Chick-fil-A; Lynsi Snyder, CEO of In-N-Out; Mary Kay Ash of Mary Kay Cosmetics; William Pollard, ServiceMaster's former CEO; and Tim Tebow and his wife, Demi-Leigh; and Charlie and Erika Kirk, Turning Point USA. Every one of these Christian business owners have lived out their faith and stewarded their finances in such a way that individuals, cities, states, nations, and the world have been transformed through the wonder-working power of Jesus Christ. They paved the road to what many believe is the next great spiritual revival in the world—outside traditional church—the marketplace.

One of the greatest World Changers for Christ was William Wilberforce, who God raised up to help abolish the slave trade in Britain. His strength came from his deep love for God and for God's way of doing business. William Wilberforce's mission ended up being the leading force in a marketplace revival and victory in the House of Commons, and it completely rescinded slave trade in the British West by 1807. As a result of Wilberforce's life-work, slave trade was totally abolished by 1833.

After the God-orchestrated victory in the House of Commons, Wilberforce was heard walking home through Hyde Park passionately praying aloud the entirety of Psalm 119. He had memorized all 176 verses! I encourage you to read all 176 verses aloud, which I've included here, to prepare your heart and mind for reading this book:

THE WAY TO HAPPINESS

You're only truly happy when you walk in total integrity, walking in the light of God's Word. What joy overwhelms everyone who keeps the ways of God, those who seek him as their heart's passion! They'll never do what's wrong but will always choose the paths of the Lord. God has prescribed the right way to live: obeying his laws with all our hearts. How I long for my life to bring you glory as I follow each and every one of your holy precepts! Then I'll never be ashamed, for I take strength from all your commandments. I will give my thanks to you from a heart of love and truth. And every time I learn more of your righteous judgments, I will be faithful to all that your Word reveals—so don't ever give up on me!

TRUE JOY

How can a young man stay pure? Only by living in the Word of God and walking in its truth. I have longed for you with the passion of my heart; don't let me stray from your directions! I consider your Word to be my greatest treasure, and I treasure it in my heart to keep me from committing sin's treason against you. My wonderful God, you are to be praised above all; teach me the power of your decrees! I speak continually of your laws as I recite out loud your counsel to me. I find more joy in following what you tell me to do than in chasing after all the wealth of the world. I set my heart on your precepts and pay close attention to all your ways. My delight is found in all your laws, and I won't forget to walk in your words.

THE ABUNDANT LIFE

Let me, your servant, walk in abundance of life that I may always live to obey your truth. Open my eyes to see the miracle-wonders hidden in Scripture. My life on earth is so brief, so tutor me in the ways of your wisdom. I am continually consumed by these irresistible longings, these cravings to obey your every commandment! Your displeasure rests with those who are arrogant, who think they know everything; you rebuke the rebellious who refuse your laws. Don't let them mock and scorn me for obeying you. For even if the princes and my leaders choose to criticize me, I will continue to serve you and walk in your plans for my life. Your commandments are my counselors; your Word is my light and delight!

REVIVED BY THE WORD

Lord, I'm fading away. I'm discouraged and lying in the dust; revive me by your word, just like you promised you would. I've poured out my life before you, and you've always been there for me. So now I ask: teach me more of your holy decrees. Open up my understanding to the ways of your wisdom, and I will meditate deeply on your splendor and your wonders. My life's strength melts away with grief and sadness; come strengthen me and encourage me with your words. Keep me far away from what is false; give me grace to stay true to your laws. I've chosen to obey your truth and walk in the splendor-light of all that you teach me. Lord, don't allow me to make a mess of my life, for I cling to your commands and follow them as closely as I can. I will run after you with delight in my heart, for you will make me obedient to your instructions.

UNDERSTANDING GOD'S WAYS

Give me revelation about the meaning of your ways so I can enjoy the reward of following them fully. Give me an understanding heart so that I can passionately know and obey your truth. Guide me into the paths that please you, for I take delight in all that you say. Cause my heart to bow before your words of wisdom and not to the wealth of this world. Help me turn my eyes away from illusions so that I pursue only that which is true; drench my soul with life as I walk in your paths. Reassure me of your promises, for I am your beloved, your servant who bows before you. Defend me from the criticism I face for keeping your beautiful words. See how I long with cravings for more of your ways? Let your righteousness revive my spirit!

TRUST IN THE LORD

May your tender love overwhelm me, O Lord, for you are my Savior and you keep your promises. I'll always have an answer for those who mock me because I trust in your word. May I never forget your truth, for I rely upon your precepts. I will observe your laws every moment of the day and will never forget the words you say. I will walk with you in complete freedom, for I seek to follow your every command. When I stand before kings, I will tell them the truth and will never be ashamed. My passion and delight is in your word, for I love what you say to me! I long for more revelation of your truth, for I love the light of your word as I meditate on your decrees.

MY COMFORT

Lord, never forget the promises you've made to me, for they are my hope and confidence. In all of my affliction I find great comfort in your promises, for they have kept me alive! No matter how bitterly the proud mockers speak against me, I refuse to budge from your precepts. Your revelation-light is eternal; I'm encouraged every time I think about your truth! Whenever I see the wicked breaking your laws, I feel horrible. As I journey through life, I put all your statutes to music; they become the theme of my joyous songs. Throughout the night I think of you, dear God; I treasure your every word to me. All this joy is mine as I follow your ways!

MY HEART IS DEVOTED TO YOU

You are my satisfaction, Lord, and all that I need, so I'm determined to do everything you say. With all my heart I seek your favor; pour out your grace on me as you promised! When I realize that I'm going astray, I turn back to obey your instructions. I give my all to follow your revelation-light; I will not delay to obey. Even when temptations encircle me with evil, I won't forget for a moment to follow your commands. In the middle of the night I awake to give thanks to you because of all your revelation-light—so right and true! Anyone who loves you and bows in obedience to your words will be my friend. Give me more revelation of your ways, for I see your love and tender care everywhere.

MY TRUE TREASURE

Your extravagant kindness to me makes me want to follow your words even more! Teach me how to make good decisions, and give me revelation-light, for I believe in your commands. Before I was humbled I used to always wander astray, but now I see the wisdom of your words. Everything you do is beautiful, flowing from your goodness; teach me the power of your wonderful words! Proud boasters make up lies about me because I am passionate to follow all that you say. Their hearts are dull and void of feelings, but I find my true treasure in your truth. The punishment you brought me through was the best thing that could have happened to me, for it taught me your ways. The words you speak to me are worth more than all the riches and wealth in the whole world!

GROWTH THROUGH THE WORD

Your very hands have held me and made me who I am; give me more revelation-light so I may learn to please you more. May all your devoted lovers see how you treat me and be glad, for your words are entwined with my heart. Lord, I know that your judgments are always right. Even when it's me you judge, you're still faithful and true. Send your kind mercy-kiss to comfort me, your servant, just like you promised you would. Love me tenderly so I can go on, for I delight in your life-giving truth. Shame upon the proud liars! See how they oppress me, all because of my passion for your precepts! May all your devoted lovers follow me as I follow the path of your instruction. Make me passionate and wholehearted to fulfill your every wish, so that I'll never have to be ashamed of myself.

DELIVER ME

I'm lovesick with yearnings for more of your salvation, for my heart is entwined with your Word. I'm consumed with longings for your promises, so I ask, "When will they all come true?" My soul feels dry and shriveled, useless and forgotten, but I will never forget your living truth. How much longer must I wait until you punish my persecutors? For I am your loving servant. Arrogant men who hate your truth and never obey your laws have laid a trap for my life. They don't know that everything you say is true, so they harass me with their lies. Help me, Lord! They've nearly destroyed my life, but I refuse to yield; I still live according to your Word. Revive me with your tender love and spare my life by your kindness, and I will continue to obey you.

FAITH IN THE WORD OF GOD

Standing firm in the heavens and fastened to eternity is the Word of God. Your faithfulness flows from one generation to the next; all that you created sits firmly in place to testify of you. By your decree everything stands at attention, for all that you have made serves you. Because your words are my deepest delight, I didn't give up when all else was lost. I can never forget the profound revelations you've taught me, for they have kept me alive more than once. Lord, I'm all yours, and you are my Savior; I have sought to live my life pleasing to you. Even though evil men wait in ambush to kill me, I will set my heart before you to understand more of your ways. I've learned that there is nothing perfect in this imperfect world except your words, for they bring such fantastic freedom into my life!

I LOVE THE WORD OF GOD

O how I love and treasure your law; throughout the day I fill my heart with its light! By considering your commands I have an edge over my enemies, for I take seriously everything you say. You have given me more understanding than those who teach me, for I've absorbed your eye-opening revelation. You have graced me with more insight than the old sages because I have not failed to walk in the light of your ways. I refused to bend my morals when temptation was before me so that I could become obedient to your Word. I refuse to turn away from difficult truths, for you yourself have taught me to love your words. How sweet are your living promises to me; sweeter than honey is your revelation-light. For your truth is the source of my understanding, not the falsehoods of those who don't know you, which I despise.

TRUTH'S SHINING LIGHT

Truth's shining light guides me in my choices and decisions; the revelation of your Word makes my pathway clear. To live my life by your righteous rules has been my holy and lifelong commitment. I'm bruised and broken, overwhelmed by it all; breathe life into me again by your living word. Lord, receive my grateful thanks and teach me more of how to please you. Even though my life hangs in the balance, I'll keep following what you've taught me, no matter what. The ungodly have done their best to throw me off track, but I'll not deviate from what you've told me to do. Everything you speak to me is like joyous treasure, filling my life with gladness. I have determined in my heart to obey whatever you say, fully and forever!

TRUST AND OBEY

I despise those who can't keep commitments, for I passionately love your revelation-light! You're my place of quiet retreat, and your wraparound presence becomes my shield as I wrap myself in your Word! Go away! Leave me, all you workers of wickedness, for you can't stop me from following every command of my God. Lord, strengthen my inner being by the promises of your Word so that I may live faithful and unashamed for you. Lift me up and I will be safe. Empower me to live every moment in the light of your ways. Lord, you reject those who reject your laws, for they fool no one but themselves! The wicked are thrown away, discarded and valueless. That's why I will keep loving all of your laws! My body trembles in holy awe of you, leaving me speechless, for I'm frightened of your righteous judgments.

I WILL FOLLOW YOUR WAYS

Don't leave me to the mercies of those who hate me, for I live to do what is just and fair. Let me hear your promise of blessing over my life, breaking me free from the proud oppressors. As a lovesick lover, I yearn for more of your salvation and for your virtuous promises. Let me feel your tender love, for I am yours. Give me more understanding of your wonderful ways. I need more revelation from your Word to know more about you, for I'm in love with you! Lord, the time has come for you to break through, for evil men keep breaking your laws. Truly, your message of truth means more to me than a vault filled with the purest gold. Every word you speak, every truth revealed, is always right and beautiful to me, for I hate what is phony or false.

I LONG TO OBEY YOU

Your marvelous words are living miracles; no wonder I long to obey everything you say. Break open your Word within me until revelation-light shines out! Those with open hearts are given insight into your plans. I open my mouth and inhale the Word of God because I crave the revelation of your commands. Turn your heart to me, Lord, and show me your grace like you do to every one of your godly lovers. Prepare before me a path filled with your promises, and don't allow even one sin to have dominion over me. Rescue me from the oppression of ungodly men so that I can keep all your precepts. Smile on me, your loving servant. Instruct me in what is right in your eyes. When I witness the rebellious breaking your laws, it makes me weep uncontrollably!

HIS WORD IS TRUE

Lord, your judgments reveal your righteousness, and your verdicts are always fair. The motive behind your every word is pure, and your teachings are remarkably faithful and true. I've been consumed with a furious passion to do what's right, all because of the way my enemies disrespect your laws. All your promises glow with fire; that's why I'm a lover of your Word. Even though I'm considered insignificant and despised by the world, I'll never abandon your ways. Your righteousness has no end; it is everlasting, and your rules are perfectly fair. Even though my troubles overwhelm me with anguish, I still delight and cherish every message you speak to me. Give me more revelation so that I can live for you, for nothing is more pure and eternal than your truth.

SAVE ME, GOD

Answer my passionate prayer, O Lord, and I'll obey everything you say. Save me, God, and I'll follow your every instruction. Before the day dawns, I'll be crying out for help and wrapping your words into my life. I lie awake every night pondering your promises to me. Lord, listen to my heart's cry, for I know your love is real for me; breathe life into me again by the revelation of your justice. Here they come—these lawless rebels are coming near, but they are all so far away from your laws. God, you are near me always, so close to me; every one of your commands reveals truth. I've known all along how true and unchanging is every word you speak, established forever!

BREATHE LIFE INTO ME AGAIN

Look upon all my misery and come be my hero to rescue me, for I will never forget what you've revealed to me. Take my side and defend me in these sufferings; redeem me and revive me, just like you promised you would. The wicked are so far from salvation, for they could not care less about your message of truth. Your tender mercies are what I need, O God; give me back my life again through the revelation of your judgments. I have so many enemies who persecute me, yet I won't swerve from following your ways. I grieve when I see how the faithless ones live, for they just walk away from your promises. Lord, see how much I truly love your instructions. So in your tender kindness, breathe life into me again. The sum total of all your words adds up to absolute truth, and every one of your righteous decrees is everlasting.

DEVOTED TO GOD'S WORD

The powerful elite have persecuted me without a cause, but my heart trembles in awe because of your miracle-words. Your promises are the source of my bubbling joy; the revelation of your Word thrills me like one who has discovered hidden treasure. I despise every lie and hate every falsehood, for I am passionate about keeping your precepts. I stop to praise you seven times a day, all because your ways are perfect! There is such a great peace and well-being that comes to the lovers of your Word, and they will never be offended. Lord, I'm longing for more of your salvation, for I want to do what pleases you. My love for your ways is indescribable; in my innermost being I want to follow them perfectly! I will keep your instructions and follow your counsel; all my ways are an open book before you.

I WANT TO FOLLOW YOU

Lord, listen to my prayer. It's like a sacrifice I bring to you; I must have more revelation of your Word! Take my words to heart when I ask you, Lord; rescue me, just like you promised! I offer you my joyous praise for all that you've taught me. Your wonderful words will become my song of worship, for everything you've commanded is perfect and true. Place your hands of strength and favor upon me, for I've made my choice to follow your ways. I wait for your deliverance, O Lord, for your words thrill me like nothing else! Invigorate my life so that I can praise you even more, and may your truth be my strength! I'll never forget what you've taught me, Lord, but when I wander off and lose my way, come after me, for I am your beloved![2]

Wilberforce had learned the most powerful example of Epic Marketplace Revival by praying scriptures from the Bible and experiencing God move Heaven and Earth when He answered his prayers to abolish slavery. God remains the same yesterday, today, and forever. His desire is for us to continuously pray the scriptures and watch Him perform miracles in the marketplace!

ONE

WHY IS MY FATHER'S BUSINESS MY MOST IMPORTANT BUSINESS?

The first recorded words in the Bible that twelve-year-old Jesus ever spoke were, "**Did you not know that I must be about My Father's business?**" When I read these important words, I wondered what Jesus meant by the words "**My Father's business**." I concluded that these words express one of the most important priorities and purposes of Jesus's life, which was to do the business of His Heavenly Father.

Family members that become involved in their family business have a tremendous responsibility along with great expectations and privileges. Representing family values and vision takes great wisdom and commitment. So many of the family members that I know in businesses like Hobby Lobby, Chick-fil-A, Shamrock Foods, and

In-N-Out Burger want to honor their families by working together with excellence.

Jesus declared that He was born to be about His Father's business. God indeed is His Father, and Jesus is His beloved Son. When Jesus talked about His Father's business, He was talking about the one and only business that will last forever throughout all eternity. That business was "all" and "only" about all things eternal. Jesus never wasted a moment of His life on things that were only temporary. Therefore, shouldn't we have as our business bottom line only things that have eternal value?

A Business Anchored In Eternity

Buildings, no matter how spectacular, never last forever. Things like diamonds are advertised that they will last forever, but the truth is they will not and cannot, because diamonds eventually degrade into graphite. Objects like clothes wear out, cars break down, electronics stop working and are discarded, shoes eventually wear thin, and even our earthly bodies wear out and decay. However, there is one thing that will never wear out: our eternal souls! Our souls, according to the Bible, will live forever.[3] Therefore, the most important business is soul business!

Investing in Souls, Not Only Sales

David Greene, the founder and CEO of Hobby Lobby, an attractive craft and decorative store, has grown his business from one store that made a first-year profit of $136.40 to 985 stores that are projected to make approximately eight billion dollars or more a year. Greene says

> Our business's bottom line should be centered around God's Word and people's souls.

his secret sauce includes making sure that his business runs on God-centered practices.[4] That means caring for souls is a top priority.

But what does it mean to care for souls? The concept of soul salvation as the real bottom line strays far from the perspective of most businesses. Yet the Bible says, "But even though grass withers and the flower fades, the word of our God stands strong forever!"[5] God's words endure forever. Does anything else? Yes. The salvation of souls! Our main business, as followers of Jesus Christ, is to let everyone know all about this good news so that we can live together forever with Jesus, who knows us best and loves us most.

In the Bible, Jesus spoke to Martha, a devoted follower, saying, "ANYONE WHO CLINGS TO ME IN FAITH, EVEN THOUGH HE DIES, WILL LIVE FOREVER. AND THE ONE WHO LIVES BY BELIEVING IN ME WILL NEVER DIE. DO YOU BELIEVE THIS?"[6] What Jesus so profoundly stated is only human souls last forever. Therefore, if our business bottom line is only things that have eternal value, and God's Word and people's souls last forever, then shouldn't our business's bottom line be centered around God's Word and people's souls?

My dad told me as a little boy, "Son, you have one life to live and it will soon be passed. Only what's done for Christ will last." Just think of taking a long look into eternity, seeing all the faces of those who are living with Christ forever, as a reward for doing business God's way!

I was humbled when God chose me to be His conduit in building and developing a nearly two-hundred acre cradle-to-grave ministry center. On this campus, we had a church building as well as a private Christian school that provided education for students in preschool to twelfth grade. We were also involved in developing a senior-living center, a medical facility, a fitness center, a multifamily housing development, an amazing residence home for young adults with special needs called Treasure House, and much more. I served for nearly forty years as the senior pastor of this amazing God-endeavor.[7] As incredible as this multimillion-dollar development is, one day it will all be gone, and only what has been and is being done for Christ will last forever!

Too many people are deceived into thinking that their legacy and greatest accomplishments are the companies they built or the buildings they created or the notoriety they achieved or the money they made, but the truth is that the only true measure of "forever success" is the people whose lives have been everlastingly transformed through salvation in Jesus Christ. The Bible emphatically states, "Believe in the Lord Jesus and you will be saved—you and all your family."[8] Just think, you and I will live forever. The question is, will you live in Heaven with

Jesus, or apart from Jesus forever? You might be asking, what does that mean? It means that while we are here on Earth, we inhabit a physical body, in an earth suit of sorts.

> A bottom line that has eternal significance will last forever!

Once we die, our physical body dies, but our soul never dies. This leads back to the choice. Will you choose Heaven or Hell?

Oh wow! This is really good news for those who surrender everything to Jesus Christ. Our choice has eternal implications. That is why this eternal promise is the one and only reason to give 100% of everything we have and everything that we do to save souls, not about how much money we can amass while on Earth. I encourage you to honestly ask yourself, am I exchanging my life for all that is eternal, or am I chasing after everything that is temporary?

The Rich Man's Question: What Must I Do?

Jesus told a powerful story in the Bible that helps us to understand how He Himself lived His life as the consummate businessperson. Jesus, the greatest businessman who walked the face of the Earth, said that every businessman and woman must wholeheartedly and enthusiastically seek after God's priority. In ancient times and today, Jesus calls all businessmen and businesswomen to develop their marketplace business with the true bottom line. A bottom line that has eternal significance will last forever!

One day a wealthy Jewish nobleman of high standing posed this question to Jesus: "Wonderful Teacher, what must I do to receive eternal life?"

Jesus answered **"Why would you call me wonderful when there is only one who is wonderful—and that is God alone? You already know what is right and what the commandments teach: 'Do not commit adultery, do not murder, do not steal, do not lie, and honor your father and your mother.'"**

The wealthy leader replied, "These are the very things I've been doing for as long as I can remember."

"**Ah**," Jesus said, "**there's still one thing you're missing in your life.**"

"What is that?" asked the man.

"**You must go and sell everything you own and give all the proceeds to the poor so you will have eternal treasures. Then come and follow me.**"

These words devastated the rich leader, for he was extremely wealthy. Jesus saw his disappointment, and looking right at him said, **"It is next to impossible for those who have everything to enter into God's kingdom. Nothing could be harder! You could**

COMPARE IT TO TRYING TO STUFF A ROPE THROUGH THE EYE OF A NEEDLE."

Those who heard this said, "Then who can be saved?"

Jesus responded, "WHAT APPEARS HUMANLY IMPOSSIBLE IS MORE THAN POSSIBLE WITH GOD. FOR GOD CAN DO WHAT MAN CANNOT."

Peter said, "Master, see how we've left all that we have, our houses and our careers, to follow you."

Jesus replied, "LISTEN TO MY WORDS: ANYONE WHO LEAVES HIS HOME BEHIND AND CHOOSES GOD'S KINGDOM OVER WIFE, CHILDREN, PARENTS, AND FAMILY, IT WILL COME BACK TO HIM MANY MORE TIMES IN THIS LIFETIME. AND IN THE AGE TO COME, HE WILL INHERIT EVEN MORE THAN THAT—HE WILL INHERIT ETERNAL LIFE!"[9]

True Life: The Eternal Reward

Imagine that . . . eternal life. Life that has no end!

Chasing after money, or anything material, ends in life's worst kind of bankruptcy. Jesus said it this way as He spoke to His disciples:[10]

IF YOU TRULY WANT TO FOLLOW ME, YOU SHOULD AT ONCE COMPLETELY REJECT AND DISOWN YOUR OWN LIFE. AND YOU MUST BE WILLING TO SHARE MY CROSS AND EXPERIENCE

IT AS YOUR OWN, AS YOU CONTINUALLY
SURRENDER TO MY WAYS. FOR IF YOU CHOOSE
SELF-SACRIFICE AND LOSE YOUR LIVES FOR MY
GLORY, YOU WILL CONTINUALLY DISCOVER TRUE
LIFE. BUT IF YOU CHOOSE TO KEEP YOUR LIVES
FOR YOURSELVES, YOU WILL FORFEIT WHAT YOU
TRY TO KEEP. FOR EVEN IF YOU WERE TO GAIN
ALL THE WEALTH AND POWER OF THIS WORLD—
AT THE COST OF YOUR OWN LIFE—WHAT GOOD
WOULD THAT BE? AND WHAT COULD BE MORE
VALUABLE TO YOU THAN YOUR OWN SOUL?
I, THE SON OF MAN, WILL ONE DAY RETURN
WITH MY MESSENGERS AND IN THE SPLENDOR
AND MAJESTY OF MY FATHER. AND THEN I WILL
REWARD EACH PERSON ACCORDING TO WHAT
THEY HAVE DONE.[11]

Going All In: A Life and Business Fully Surrendered

In other words, God is calling us to Himself. God will
never leave us or forsake us. Just know that God is on our
side, by our side, and inside twenty-four hours a day, seven
days a week, 365 days a year, forever and ever and ever.
One might ask, "Did Jesus really say to offer yourselves up
to death?" This had to be ridiculously shocking. Everyone
must honestly answer, "What would I be willing to give

up, or give in to, in exchange for my life?" Answering those questions will determine your eternal destiny.

If you've chosen to follow Christ at the cost of your own life, this will include the way you do business. And since you are still reading this book, you are probably ready to go all in. After over fifty years of doing business God's way, I've discovered some key essential values that will create an eternal and compelling workplace for your Christ-centered business.

The Epic Marketplace Revival Values

Value #1: Develop A Winsome & Winning Attitude

What is meant by "winsome" or "winning" in the marketplace and doing it God's way? These two powerful words of application are necessary to create an atmosphere of joy and encouragement to all those around you. Having a winsome and winning attitude means having the wisdom to extend grace, even if it does not feel like the best "business" choice. In Proverbs, it says, "Winsome words pour from a heart of wisdom, adding value to all you teach."[12] Marketplace winsomeness is essential as well as an irresistible magnet for

> Winsome attitudes, respectful relationships, love-driven workplaces, generous habits, joy-filled conversations, unity, and enthusiasm—essential values for Christ-centered enterprises.

maintaining loyal employees, attracting customers and retaining them.

Create a winsome atmosphere by developing a winning attitude with your staff, your customers, your vendors, and your suppliers as well as with anyone else with whom you have the privilege of interacting within your business.

Paul encourages us to stick close to Jesus, who is the Master of Winsomeness. Without an alignment with Jesus, it is impossible to extend a winsome and winning attitude.

> Look at how much encouragement you've found in your relationship with the Anointed One! You are filled to overflowing with his comforting love. You have experienced a deepening friendship with the Holy Spirit and have felt his tender affection and mercy.
>
> So I am asking you, my friends, that you be joined together in perfect unity—with one heart, one passion, and united in one love. Walk together with one harmonious purpose and you will fill my heart with unbounded joy.
>
> Be free from pride-filled opinions, for they will only harm your cherished unity. Don't allow self-promotion to hide in your hearts, but in authentic humility put others first and view others as more important than yourselves.

Abandon every display of selfishness. Possess a greater concern for what matters to others instead of your own interests.

And consider the example that Jesus, the Anointed One, has set before us. Let his mindset become your motivation.[13]

Value #2: Cultivate Respectful Relationships

Each person longs to be respected and honored. Every word spoken and every action taken matters! Our words and actions either promote respect and honor, or they disparage one another. Honor and respect are mandates from God, as shown in 1 Timothy 6:1–2.

Instruct every employee to respect and honor their employers, for this attitude presents to them a clear testimony of God's truth and renown. Tell them to never provide them with a reason to discredit God's name because of their actions. Especially honor and respect employers who are believers and don't despise them, but serve them even more, for they are fellow believers. They should be at peace with them as beloved members of God's family. Be faithful to teach them these things as their sacred obligation.

Value #3: Design a Love-Driven Workplace

Many have heard the love chapter quoted at weddings but never think of applying it to their work environment. The love section of the Bible emphatically emphasizes that the greatest of these values is love. Do not underestimate a loving workplace environment as a place that inspires your employees to align with the vision and focus to share God's love not only internally and but to customers.

Love is large and incredibly patient. Love is gentle and consistently kind to all. It refuses to be jealous when blessing comes to someone else. Love does not brag about one's achievements, nor inflate its own importance. Love does not traffic in shame and disrespect, nor selfishly seek its own honor. Love is not easily irritated or quick to take offense. Love joyfully celebrates honesty and finds no delight in what is wrong. Love is a safe place of shelter, for it never stops believing the best for others. Love never takes failure as defeat, for it never gives up. Love never stops loving.[14]

Every business needs to create a genuinely unconditional, nonjudgmental, loving workplace environment that will cement the foundation for doing business God's way.

Value #4: Build generous hearts and habits.

What exactly does building generous hearts and habits mean? Does it mean developing generosity in your business? Are gifts always tangible and monetary? Absolutely not. Gifts can be tangible; however, generosity also means pouring your talents into another person—mentoring, teaching, and training them in God's ways of conducting business. It can mean parsing out wisdom to another person in your organization or industry.

In Luke, Jesus says, "**GIVE GENEROUSLY AND GENEROUS GIFTS WILL BE GIVEN BACK TO YOU, SHAKEN DOWN TO MAKE ROOM FOR MORE. ABUNDANT GIFTS WILL POUR OUT UPON YOU WITH SUCH AN OVERFLOWING MEASURE THAT IT WILL RUN OVER THE TOP! THE MEASUREMENT OF YOUR GENEROSITY BECOMES THE MEASUREMENT OF YOUR RETURN.**"[15]

Have you ever known a person who was generous in spirit? Someone who was willing to help others, even go out of their way for others, expecting nothing in return? God is the one who rewards generosity. Proverbs is a book in the Bible with exceptional wisdom meant to offer guidance in conducting everyday affairs. The authorship is attributed to King Solomon, who was considered the wisest man who ever lived. In Proverbs, there is great wisdom about generosity, "Generosity brings prosperity, but withholding from charity brings poverty."[16] The Greek word used in the original text for *Charity* can also be translated as love.

In the very next verse, this wise man tells us, "Those who live to bless others will have blessings heaped upon them, and the one who pours out his life to pour out blessings will be saturated with favor."[17] Wow! What an amazing return on investment (ROI). The entire book of Proverbs is rich with wisdom. With thirty-one chapters in Proverbs, leaders can infuse their days with incredible wisdom by reading one chapter each day—aligning life, business, and decision-making with God's insights. In doing so, one would learn important keys to godly success, not just the world's standard of success. In Proverbs it says, "But a life lived loving God bears lasting fruit, for the one who is truly wise wins souls."[18]

Value #5: Lead with Joy-Filled Conversations

When I pastored that very large church in Arizona, I would begin our worship time together the same way my mother began every morning of my life. She would walk into the room, open up the shades and say, "This is the day that the Lord has made—we're going to rejoice and be glad in it." Oh, what a great way to jumpstart a joyful day.

As I grew up, I recorded that verse, Psalm 118:24, on my telephone's answering service and also recorded the joyful words from Nehemiah 8:10, "The joy of the Lord is my strength." When God is by my side and inside me, there's really no reason not to have continuous joyful conversations.

Joy isn't a mood—it's momentum. Spirit-filled leaders spark contagious conversations that lift hearts, unify teams, and inspire purpose. When God dwells within, joy becomes your default—steady in meetings, resilient in setbacks, and radiant in the face of pressure.

Use every opportunity to cultivate joy.

Value #6: Let Unity Be Your Competitive Advantage

Throughout scripture, God is very clear when he addresses kingdoms that will not survive. Thomas Reid, an eighteenth-century religious philosopher, coined the popular phrase still used today, "A chain is only as strong as its weakest link." It is likely that Reid took this from the Bible, where Jesus clearly states, "No kingdom can endure if it is divided against itself."[19]

God pours out uncontainable blessings when we are unified, as said in Psalm 133:1, "How truly wonderful and delightful it is to see brothers and sisters living together in sweet unity!" In the same Psalm, God then goes further by saying how precious unity can be, as precious as sacred oil flowing down to cleanse us, heal us, restore us and invigorate our entire being! Amid it all, we receive a blessed life that goes beyond what we can even dream or imagine possible when we are unified.

In order for a business or organization to be successful, it must be aligned and unified in its direction and mission. Whether leading a global enterprise or a small team, your organization's strength lies in its alignment. Build unity with intentionality, humility, and shared mission because in the Kingdom, agreement unlocks blessings. In the marketplace, it unlocks momentum.

Value #7: Ignite Enthusiasm!

I love the word *enthusiasm*. *Enthusiasm* is the Greek word *Entheos*, meaning "full of God!" Enthusiasm is incredibly contagious! I love to tell people to go and change the world with enthusiasm!

There was a time, during my forty years as the senior pastor at Community Church of Joy that our church was growing rapidly, and many people started to tell their friends, who told their friends, who told their friends, and so on. The church got so crowded that we needed to build more buildings, especially for children to learn about Jesus and for the community to know what it means to fall more deeply in love with Jesus and follow Him. In order to expand, we needed the support of the surrounding neighborhood. I found myself starting a building campaign where I had to go door-to-door around the neighborhood that surrounded the church asking our neighbors for their permission to expand.

At the end of our campus, there was an athletic field. In front of that was a row of houses. I knocked on one particular homeowner's door and the person that answered was a leather-clad, biker-tough man.

I introduced myself and the purpose for knocking on his door.

He greeted me by saying, "I don't know what happens in that place . . . but every Sunday, people walk in quiet and leave skipping toward their cars . . . driving away like wild stallions breaking free."

Then he looked me in the eye and said, "What in the world happens inside your church that causes people to get so excited?"

I was then privileged to tell him that the secret to an enthusiastic life was Christ alone!

Enthusiasm isn't hype—it's holy. Enthusiasm means letting God fill up every place and every space in our lives. It gives us eternal perspective, shifts atmospheres, and causes businesses to run with purpose, not just profit. It envelops our thoughts, our attitudes, and our conversations. When that happens, there is uncontainable joy filled with enthusiasm! Enthusiasm bursts us open for the desire to live and do business God's way. Business done God's way will always be done according to God's will.

In 1 John 2:15–17, the Bible tells us this:

Don't set the affections of your heart on this world or in loving the things of the world. The love of the Father and the love of the world are incompatible. For all that the world can offer us—the gratification of our flesh, the allurement of things of the world, and the obsession with status and importance—none of these things come from the Father but from the world. This world and its desires are in the process of passing away, but those who love to do the will of God live forever.

Join the Revival: Who Will You Invite?

Imagine if your business and my business were focused like a laser beam on habitually and continuously doing the will of God. As Jesus Himself confirmed, that's His purpose—to do the will of the Heavenly Father. That looks a lot like going to work every day overflowing with enthusiasm that will ignite a passion within you to become a part of the unstoppable Epic Marketplace Revival!

Ask yourself: Who am I going to invite to join me in being a courageous champion to help lead the unstoppable Epic Marketplace Revival?

TWO

For the one who is truly wise wins souls.
Proverbs 11:30

KEEP SHARPLY FOCUSED ON SAVING ONE SOUL AT A TIME

I once heard a story about a young boy walking along the beach with his daddy when he saw multiple starfish that had washed up on shore. Without skipping a beat, the little boy began to throw them, one at a time, back into the ocean.

His daddy said softly, "Son, you cannot save them all."

As the little boy threw one more into the ocean, he looked back to his daddy and said, "But I can at least save this one!"

What is the value of saving one soul?

A Priceless Valuation

In 2013, Walt Hickey wrote an article for Business Insider entitled, "We Calculated How Much Your Soul Is

Actually Worth." In the article, he concluded, as it relates to money, that a soul is worth four million dollars. Four million dollars in 2013 is worth approximately five and a half million in 2025. However, God's calculation of a soul is priceless. In fact, it was so priceless that He chose to sacrifice His Son's life and shed His blood on a cross to save every soul.

As a pastor of over forty years, I encountered multitudes of people who regularly came to church simply to find relief. They were selling out their expectations way too cheaply! Jesus came into the world to change the world, not simply to offer relief to people who only wanted to fix up their old lives. Christ wants so much

> Every soul is priceless—validated by the sacrifice of Christ.

more for His beloved people. The Bible says, "Now, if anyone is enfolded into Christ, he has become an entirely new person. All that is related to the old order has vanished. Behold, everything is fresh and new. And God has made all things new."[20] Christ eagerly wants to give everyone who is willing a new life in exchange for their old life. Wow! No more trying to fix up the old life.

Everyone who asks gets a brand-new life, because Jesus Christ makes everything brand new! Christ makes us new in every way—mentally, emotionally, physically, spiritually, and financially. The good news is, with Jesus we become new people. People with new ideas, new ethics, and new values. God eagerly wants to do a new thing individually, as well as corporately in the marketplace.

New Garments, New Wineskin

Jesus illustrates our new life by teaching us that no one rips up a new garment to make a patch for an old, worn-out garment. If you tear up the new garment to patch the old one, it will eventually tear the old garment even more. Have you ever heard the story of the wine merchant receiving new wine, but he was too cheap to put it in a new wineskin? The old wineskin had already been saturated and was weak and worn out, so you can only imagine what happened next. If you guessed the new wine leaked out, you would be correct! The new wine burst the old skin, and he lost all the wine.[21]

I have heard and said the only one that welcomes change is a wet baby, and even then, there are tears and screams and cries for help, resisting change. Change is hard. It is easier sometimes to insist on doing things the same way and stick with the familiar. People will often say they know what they like, but what that really means is they like what they know. Resisting change can lead to the loss of companies and sometimes even health and marriages.

Guarding Against Greed

As my wife, Blakney, and I remain sharply Kingdom-focused, we understand that economizing and scaling back require large changes in our spending habits in addition to our financial attitudes and behaviors toward money. Jesus is clear when He tells the people in Luke 12:15 to guard your hearts from greed and to stop wishing for what you do not possess. Our hearts remain passionate about rightsizing our finances and downsizing the things that we have already acquired. This change for us has not been easy, but it has been worth it, because to obey is better than sacrifice.[22]

> Doing business God's way isn't easy—but it's always the *"worth it way."*

Jesus calls everyone to wholeheartedly seek after the things that are permanent instead of working harder and harder to acquire more temporary "things" or "stuff." God calls those who spend their daily lives in the marketplace to be Christ's ambassadors in that arena. Marketplace disruptors are to be agents of change. God wants us to keep our focus on the ultimate grand prize, which God calls the victorious permanent prize. That prize is living together forever with Jesus, our Savior, in our new, Heavenly dwelling place.

Paul: Marketplace Ambassador

One of my marketplace heroes is the apostle Paul. Paul encourages every Christian businessperson in order to grow a successful marketplace business God's way, each person must wholeheartedly run the race God sets before them.[23] He also demonstrated what it meant to follow Christ. He was beaten and thrown in prison numerous times. Yet he claimed it was all worth it. Paul said, "For to me, to live is Christ, and to die is gain."[24] Paul's eyes were fixed on all things eternal, meaning if he lived, he would tell everyone of Christ's love and sacrifice; but if he died, he would be with Christ in eternity. Living this way, Paul knew following Christ was worth it. Doing business God's way, and living according to His plan, will *never* be the easy way, yet Jesus promises that it will be the "worth it way."

Whenever Blakney and I as a couple have the opportunity to listen to leading business leaders, the popular entrepreneurs in the marketplace, or the power brokers who seem to be continuously successful, most of them admit that they truly failed their way forward. Many of their failures and difficulties forced them to question if it was really all worth it. I've been told many stories of significant loss, pain, and suffering from discouragement. There are volumes of books, articles, and documentaries that talk about the emptiness and loneliness from chasing after the temporary. Jesus tells us that because of a gracious God, failure never has to be final, nor does failure have to be a fatal verdict, because Jesus always has the final word, and it will be good! No matter the difficulty, successfully doing business God's way always pleases God!

Paul was commissioned by Jesus to go into the marketplace and win souls for God. Paul, who had a radical transformation from persecuting Christians to wanting to save souls for Jesus, funded his own calling to the mission field. He continued to be a successful businessman in order to fund his travels to tell the world about Jesus. In fact, this consummate businessman wrote most of the New Testament. Paul was an early pioneer in the Epic Marketplace Revival movement.

One business that Paul was instrumental in helping shut down was the business of making figures of false idols to worship. These figures were made out of wood, stone and metal. The companies that made these false idols sold them for large amounts of profits. These false godlike figures only left people feeling more broken, afraid, and empty. Even though this certainly was a very prosperous business, Paul knew the truth about this business, and that it was leading people away from God. False idols were created by the devil to destroy life instead of building up an abundant life.

Because of Paul's obedience to this revival, multitudes of businessmen's and businesswomen's lives became radically transformed by the wonder-working power of Jesus Christ. When Paul did business in the marketplace, they were helped mentally, emotionally, physically, spiritually, and even financially.

Paul learned this "way of doing business" by personally knowing Jesus, the King of the marketplace. The reality is that Jesus must be Lord *in* the marketplace since He is already Lord *of* the marketplace. Today's culture believes that business and Jesus should be kept separate in order to be successful; however, the businessman-apostle Paul took a radical stance for Christ in the marketplace.

Keeping Jesus out of the marketplace is a recipe for disaster due to the fact Christians are called to stand strong and be courageous as well as bold, always seeking to do business God's way. We are also called to contribute to discipling and helping God's marketplace dwellers to become fully devoted to doing business God's way!

One day a group of business leaders from the city banded together and kicked the apostle Paul out of the city. However, Paul boldly continued sharing the good news of a transformed life through the power of Jesus Christ. Paul taught people the worthlessness of gods made by people's handiwork and how everyone needed to adore and worship the only true God, who was the source of abundant living and eternal life. He passionately preached on how to save the very souls of the people who were lost in the city. Paul knew the reality that how the city goes, so goes the state, and eventually so goes the world. For what do you truly gain in your business if your business thrives, yet your city rejects Christ?

True Profit or Loss

What does it profit when someone builds a successful business yet loses their city, state, or nation for Christ? This thought was in my head when I worked diligently and prayed fervently to build a great multigenerational church campus. I intentionally and strategically connected with many businesses in the community. I built friendships with key businessmen and businesswomen in our greater Phoenix area. Countless days I'd wake up asking the question, "What would it truly profit me if I built a great church, yet the city was lost?" That burning question lit a fire in my heart driving me to fervently work and pray for a revival to take place in the marketplace. Everything we could ever endeavor to accomplish is rubbish compared to the infinite value of knowing Jesus Christ, the Lord. For this, I have disregarded everything else and count it all garbage, so that I could gain Christ and become one with him.[25]

> Lord, lay some soul upon my heart and love that soul through me; and may I nobly do my part to win that soul for Thee! —Leon Tucker

I discovered that once again the true, bottom line must be measured not in dollars and cents or even in peoples' achievements, rather the significant bottom line must be measured not by temporary but eternal treasures. God tells us that every material thing we could ever want to hang on to will either be destroyed by rust or eaten by moths; only what is eternal will last forever.[26]

In our lives, we can only give away what we have; we cannot give away what we do not have. If our lives are empty, and we don't have purpose and meaning as well as love, joy, peace, patience, goodness, kindness, gentleness, faithfulness, and self-control, we are not able to help other people. We must learn how to live God's way in order to do business God's way. Our business can only grow to the level we have grown in our own God-guided leadership and our own lives. God wants us to think about what is authentic and what is real, what is honorable, what is admirable, what is beautiful and respectful, what is pure and holy, what is merciful and kind, and God calls us to fasten our thoughts on every glorious work He is doing, praising Him always! We are commanded to put into practice all that we have heard or seen! Then the God of peace will be with us in all things, so we surrender everything to live like Jesus lived, love like Jesus loved, lead like Jesus led, and do what Jesus has done, is doing, and will continue to do. My friend, God's way is true success that leads to an Epic Marketplace Revival.

My challenge to you is to pray earnestly, "Lord, lay some soul upon my heart and love that soul through me; and may I nobly do my part to win that soul for Thee!" (Leon Tucker, 1939).

Ask yourself this: How am I willing to ignite a marketplace revival in my own community?

THREE

You are the average of the five people you spend
the most time with.
Jim Rohn

YOU SHOW THAT YOU ARE MY INTIMATE FRIENDS
WHEN YOU OBEY ALL THAT I COMMAND YOU.
I HAVE NEVER CALLED YOU 'SERVANTS,' BECAUSE
A MASTER DOESN'T CONFIDE IN HIS SERVANTS,
AND SERVANTS DON'T ALWAYS UNDERSTAND
WHAT THE MASTER IS DOING. BUT I CALL YOU
MY MOST INTIMATE AND CHERISHED FRIENDS,
FOR I REVEAL TO YOU EVERYTHING THAT I'VE
HEARD FROM MY FATHER.
John 15:14–15

CHOOSE YOUR INNER CIRCLE WISELY!

Jim Rohn, an influential marketplace entrepreneur, author, motivational coach, and speaker, said the number one book a successful person should read is the Bible. He also said that who a person surrounds themself with will tell a lot about the character and heart of that person.

Some of the questions we all should be asking ourselves as we seek to do business God's way are these:

- Who are the five people within your inner circle?
- Who has the most influence on you personally?
- Who is influencing your business decisions?
- Who are your mentors?
- Who are your coaches?
- Who is discipling you?
- Who is teaching you?
- Who is leading your company?
- Who are you partnering with in business?

- Who are your friends and confidants?
- Who are the TV personalities that you follow?
- What television shows do you watch?
- What movies do you go to?
- Who are your media personalities that you listen to?
- Who are your favorite authors?
- Who are you reading?

Questions for Reflection

In other words, how much influence do others have on your ability to do business God's way versus how much influence does what God says about life and business have on your ability to do it His way? Whoever and whatever captures your attention and fills your thoughts most of the time has the most influence and power over you. God is very clear when He instructs us to seek God's Kingdom first and all the rest will fall into place.[27] He also instructs us to meditate on His Word day and night.[28]

Godly Mentors and Models

In the Bible, we are given great wisdom and guidance to help us choose who are the best "whos" for our inner circle. God really cares about our choice of who! However, this has to start with our relationship with Christ. He always needs to be the most important *WHO* in our life.

If we are not spending time with Him and not reading scripture, we cannot hear from Him and be led by the Holy Spirit to make wise choices for our inner circle. We succumb to the world's enticements and lures to be "popular," to be "liked," to even be "rich." As a result, there are many times in our lives we are unable to choose wisely the "whos" in our lives.

In the Bible, God explicitly tells us who He desires His people to turn to for the greatest guidance, counseling, and direction! God encourages us to look for winsome, God-honoring examples. God's choice for our "who" shares eternal values, eternal virtues, and eternal morals in order to pour into us with supernatural wisdom and knowledge. These attributes are essential for having eternal success in choosing God's ideal who.

The apostle Paul, a marketplace tentmaker in the Bible and one of my influential voices, had a lot to say about building a business that would ignite an Epic Marketplace Revival! In fact, he's written the greatest number of books in the Bible about doing everything God's way! In chapter 1, we previously looked at Philippians 2:1–5 where Paul encouraged those in the marketplace to look to Jesus as their example. Paul expounds on the importance of not only how to conduct ourselves in the marketplace but how to draw closer to Christ for His guidance on how to conduct our whole life God's way.

When we are gathering our inner circle of our five persons, as Jim Rohn calls it, we must look for those who are biblically guided and influenced by Jesus in their own life. We must make sure they are firmly planted in changing the marketplace for Christ and that winning souls is more important to them than their financial bottom line. Are they seeking to live their life God's way, and do they seek to do business God's way?

This application would be relevant to choosing business coaches. Too many executives and business leaders are looking at the conventional, corporate way of doing business. Those coaches may know how to create a P&L statement (profits and loss) but walking with Jesus is the furthest thing from their mind. They are usually financially motivated and not Kingdom focused. While you may gain helpful information on business tactics, be careful you do not get caught up in their way of *not* doing business God's way. In order to be in alignment with God for your marketplace assignment, it is crucial to be in the Word of God and to always guard your heart and mind with the information received daily by engaging in biblical truths, truths that are God-honoring, God-pleasing, and wisdom-infused. What needs to have the final word on all your business decisions is the impact that is made for eternal success.

The apostle Paul tells us:

My beloved ones, just like you've always listened to everything I've taught you in the past, I'm asking you now to keep following my instructions as though I were right there with you. Now you must continue to make this new life fully manifested as you live in the holy awe of God—which brings you trembling into his presence. God will continually revitalize you, implanting within you the passion to do what pleases him.[29]

Then he goes on to remind us that we need to be a shining light like the light of Christ, "holding out the words of *eternal* life."[30] As Kingdom entrepreneurs, we must let our light shine before others, so the marketplace businesses see our good works—not as mere success stories, but as living examples of eternity pursued and Heaven's promises embraced.

Character, Chemistry & Competence

After interacting with multitudes of marketplace leaders around the world, I discovered a truth: hiring those with the right heart, gifts, attitude, and skills comes down to three essentials—character, chemistry, and competence. These aren't just business traits; they're Kingdom filters that reveal who's equipped to walk with vision and steward legacy.

Character

The first ingredient is godly character. God-honoring character is essential. As I staffed what became one hundred and fifty people, I would always search for men and women of Christlike character that generated great integrity, great honesty, and great trustworthiness. It was extremely important to have their words match how they lived.

Chemistry

The second most important quality or ingredient is chemistry. The right chemistry begins with healthy inter-personal relationships, which produce a joyful, positive attitude. Although generally not tangible, chemistry is that ability to interact with those where conversations flow easily, and there is an air of effortless collaboration of ideas. As I evaluated this quality, I would search for people that lived their lives in harmony with others, whether in private, in public, at work, or at home. Since there are no solo successes in a team, having a servant's heart and building commitment is essential. A team player always enjoys the success of helping people discover God's purpose and plans for their life.

> **Three key essentials for Kingdom-minded leadership: Character, Chemistry, Competence**

Competence

The third but equally important ingredient is competence. Talent cannot be ignored! I would look for people who were eager, ready, and willing to apply and improve their talent. They may not have taken their talents to their highest ability or be fully mature yet but will do "whatever it takes" to improve their skill set.

In addition to character, chemistry, and competence, it is important to examine examples of Jesus's inner circle and how He chose His disciples, who ended up changing the world. These disciples had God-sized passionate hearts to please God in all things. It is important to always ask God, "Are you pleased?"

My question to you today is, Who is on your team? What champions are you pursuing to join you in not only making a difference but in creating a different world, where people are laser focused on what's permanent, not just on things that are temporary?

One of the most successful businesspersons I admire and appreciate is Ken Blanchard. One afternoon while I was riding with him in his car out of San Diego, he said to me, "Always hire for heart and train for skill." Yes, that's exactly God's way of building a successful Epic Marketplace Business.

Heart Over Hype

The Bible refers to the heart more than one thousand times. In Proverbs 3:5, the writer, King Soloman, says "Trust in the Lord completely, and do not rely on your own opinions. With all your heart rely on him to guide you, and he will lead you in every decision you make." Then in the next verse, he tells us to "become intimate with him in whatever you do, and he will lead you wherever you go."[31] The next sentence instructs us, "Don't think for a moment that you know it all, for wisdom comes when you adore him with undivided devotion and avoid everything that's wrong."[32] Finally, in verse 8 it expresses that if you heed these instructions, you will find the great healing refreshment that your body and spirit long for. As Solomon wraps up the section in Proverbs 3, entitled "Wisdom's Guidance," he tells us to glorify God with all our wealth, honoring him with our very best, with every increase that comes to us; as we do, our lives will overflow with magnificent blessings from an uncontainable source of inner joy.[33]

One of the keys to unlocking great truths, is found when Jesus says, **"LOVE THE LORD YOUR GOD WITH EVERY PASSION OF YOUR HEART, WITH ALL THE ENERGY OF YOUR BEING, AND WITH EVERY THOUGHT THAT IS WITHIN YOU."**[34] Jesus also said there was a second key, **"AND THE SECOND IS LIKE IT IN IMPORTANCE: 'YOU MUST LOVE YOUR FRIEND IN THE SAME WAY YOU LOVE YOURSELF.'"**[35] In my years in the marketplace, I have found that a loving, tender, supple heart is at the core of all eternally-minded successful people. Just imagine in your workplace if everyone loved the way Jesus loved, by laying their life down for you.

> **Always hire for heart and train for skill.**
> **—Ken Blanchard**

Imagine if the staff members of your marketplace business always practiced Jesus's sacrificial love for other employees and customers, and even more amazing would be if everyone was trying to outdo one another with their love. The whole world would beat a path to your business. We have been personally chosen by God Himself to go into the world and be fruitfully prosperous in terms of eternal value. God would be so pleased to see more love, more joy, more peace, more patience, more goodness, more kindness, more gentleness, more faithfulness, and more self-control.

How many businesses do you know that operate wholeheartedly and enthusiastically with the purpose and passion to know and be known by their unstoppable love? When a business exists for its own benefit and is first and foremost

> God, are You pleased with me?

financially driven, employees as well as customers will soon become resentful about the way business is done and walk away, never to return. Being all about economics demonstrates that everyone and everything else is of lesser value and importance than profit. Soon the reputation becomes "all the company cares about is money." The business will be labeled greedy, and this negative reputation will be gossiped to the point that customers will lose respect, and you will lose good customers. That foundation is weak and will crumble. Its impact diminishes any effort to build a successful community around it.

On the other hand, every business that is eternally, zealously, and generously driven will build a healthy, thriving community around them that will successfully give birth to a God honoring business igniting an Epic Marketplace Revival movement.

Ask yourself this: Who are within my inner circle of "whos," and why have I chosen them? Is Jesus my most important who? Why or why not?

FOUR

Any temporal possession can be turned into everlasting wealth. Whatever is given to Christ is immediately touched with immortality.
AW Tozer

GIVE GENEROUSLY AND GENEROUS GIFTS WILL BE GIVEN BACK TO YOU, SHAKEN DOWN TO MAKE ROOM FOR MORE.
Luke 6:38

GROW A SILVER-DOLLAR ATTITUDE AND AN ETERNALLY FOCUSED HEART AND MIND

I discovered as a seven-year-old how much uncontainable joy and incredible delight I got from giving generously and sacrificially. I remember my very first silver dollar. I gripped it tightly in the palm of my hand. I had been given the silver dollar as a gift for riding along as a passenger in a Model T Ford in the Lakefield, Minnesota, city summer parade. When I got home, I burst through the front door with an enthusiastic announcement, "I'm home and I'm rich!"

I held in my hand more money than I had ever imagined I could possibly accumulate as a seven-year-old. I deposited the money in my room and eagerly waited for Sunday church to roll around. My three sisters along with my mom and dad were very curious to see what I would do with the silver dollar. As I got ready to go to church, I made sure to put my silver dollar in my pocket.

As the offering plate was passed, I gleefully placed the shiny silver dollar into the plate! Immediately, my mother and sisters gasped!

Mom whispered to me, "What are you doing? Are you giving it all to Jesus?"

With a big God-sized smile, I said, "Yep."

The feeling I had inside of me was uncontainable joy! At that moment, I discovered one of the greatest feelings I could ever have, and one I have carried with me throughout my life, it is the feeling that comes when you give generously and sacrificially.

God's Ownership

One of my life-changing discoveries has been that I can never outgive God. The reality is that God owns it all in the first place. Tim Keller said, "A lack of generosity refuses to acknowledge that your assets are not really yours, but God's."[36] Everything I have or ever will have belongs to God! Psalm 24:1 says, "The earth is the Lord's and everything in it." As I pondered the depth of this verse, it clearly means that God owns absolutely everything. When I gave my silver dollar to Jesus, it belonged to Him in the first place. God is always the most generous of anyone.

Outrageous Giving

My wife, Blakney, came to me one day and asked me to pray about how much, as a couple, we were going to sacrificially give away as our tithes and offerings. This inspired both of us to think bigger and pray harder than we had thought or prayed before. The wisdom of Proverbs challenged us as God clearly said He loves a cheerful giver,[37] and those that are generous will prosper.[38] We both prayed earnestly asking God, "What amount do You desire from us?" As our faith and trust grows, the generosity quotient (GQ) grows.

> A lack of generosity refuses to acknowledge that your assets are not really yours, but God's.
> —Tim Keller

God has clearly stated to all of us that once we understand it is all His, He will be asking each of us to become outrageous givers. Generosity is not just monetary, it includes time, and talents too. The truth is that generous giving leads to generous living, which leads to a greater heart of generosity. My wife and I strive to live by these principles and seek wholeheartedly to become outrageous givers. Our primary purpose in being generous is to advance His Kingdom. The cry of our hearts is to see all precious souls on Earth won over to Jesus Christ and see them enthusiastically and wholeheartedly follow, love, serve, thank, praise, enjoy, trust, and please Him!

He Gave Everything

One of the most beloved verses in the Bible is the salvation verse. In John 3:16, Jesus said, "FOR HERE IS THE WAY GOD LOVED THE WORLD—HE GAVE HIS ONLY, UNIQUE SON AS A GIFT. SO NOW EVERYONE WHO BELIEVES IN HIM WILL NEVER PERISH BUT EXPERIENCE EVERLASTING LIFE." God has provided each of us with sufficient resources and everything we need to bring the good news of salvation in Jesus to the whole world. Everything we'll ever need to be saved for eternity comes from surrendering everything to Jesus.[39] God's Son, Jesus Christ, knows that the greatest and most important days of our lives will come when we transition from today's abundant life here on Earth to an eternal life in Heaven. That's why I have chosen not to prioritize pursuing anything temporary, which will never completely satisfy anyway. Eventually our lives on Earth will come to an end. However, our forever lives in Heaven will never end. A forever life is everlasting. That means there are no limits of time or space. There will be no sickness, sorrow, or death. Our eternal lives will be permanent. One thousand years will seem like a day.

Gift Wrapped in Eternity

One day, a couple was discussing how time in Heaven is measured. One of them said a thousand years on Earth is like a day in Heaven. A few days later, the couple was complaining that it seemed God took so long to answer their prayers. So they decided to ask God why that was. God replied, "Just give me a day!"

The point of this fun story is that Heaven's timing is perfect, based on the timeline of eternity. Eternity will last forever and ever! That is why we must always keep our focus on everything eternal and not on temporary things. When Jesus taught His disciples to pray one of the most well-known prayers in the biblical worldview, He concluded with these words: "FOR YOURS IS THE KINGDOM AND THE POWER AND THE GLORY FOREVER. AMEN."[40] What is so amazing is that we will have a new, perfect, eternal body as we live out our eternal lives. The Greek word for everlasting life means perpetual. According to the Bible, we are all created in the image of God, which makes us spiritual beings inside our human bodies. That makes us spiritual bodies having a human experience.

When my earthly body dies, it will decay. Nevertheless, my soul will live on forever and ever.

In the Bible, it tells us that Jesus's business was to fill our lives, including our hearts and minds, with eternal wisdom.[41] We were made to never settle for anything less than God's eternal best. It's incredibly amazing how God is able to take all our possessions, whether material possessions or financial possessions or God-given talents and abilities, and multiply them into everlasting success.

A pastor many years ago, A. W. Tozer, once said that whatever we give to Christ, such as our time, talents, and money, it is immediately touched and wrapped in eternity. Just think, your whole life is jam packed with all the God-given talents, abilities, finances, and every other resource that has the potential to contribute to not only making a difference but to actually making a different world that touches eternity. If we will only surrender our lives.

Life on Earth is no more than temporary. Abundant life is overflowing with eternal promises. How does that make you feel? God made you and me for Himself. This actually connects God's people to eternity. Wherever we work, we are literally the hands and feet of Jesus, who is the Savior of the world.

Kingdom-Crafted Purpose

Paul, who wrote most of the books of the New Testament, fourteen to be exact, was a very successful entrepreneur and artisan as a skilled tent maker. One ordinary day, he had a massive, life-changing encounter with God. In an instant he became one thousand times committed

> **God made you and me for Himself.**

to everything eternal. I love the words Paul uses to paint a picture of the people who are earnestly seeking God as well as an eternal destiny with their family, friends, and marketplace associates in Heaven forever.

Paul says, "We have become his poetry, a recreated people that will fulfill the destiny he has given each of us, for we are joined to Jesus, the Anointed One. Even before we were born, God planned in advance our destiny and the good works we would do to fulfill it!"[42] Just imagine God choosing you and me to do good works that would be a part of His eternal plan. What God chooses for good will last through all eternity. It will be permanent. It will not fade away like all temporary things do.

Honestly, our time here on Earth is very brief. We want to make the most of every day, living out the greatest adventure of a lifetime. How thrilling life becomes as we regularly experience God's amazing miracles.

Jesus said, "WHILE I AM WITH YOU, IT IS DAYTIME AND WE MUST DO THE WORKS OF GOD WHO SENT ME WHILE THE LIGHT SHINES. FOR THERE IS COMING A DARK NIGHT WHEN NO ONE WILL BE ABLE TO WORK."[43] This truth says that we are called to live wholeheartedly committed to focusing on all things eternal.

Some years ago, a friend of mine, Bob Buford, who succeeded extravagantly in business, told me that when he gets to Heaven, God will ask him to answer two questions. The first question will be "Do you love me?" The second question that will follow is "Who did you bring with you?" It does matter to God what's done for Christ with our life. We will be held accountable on Judgment Day. Accountability will come in how we invest our time, talents, and treasures on Earth into God's main mission.

A Redeemed Investor

Accountability is firmly stated in the Bible through the story of a little man named Zacchaeus. Zacchaeus was a high-ranking, wealthy supervisor of all the tax collectors in the region. One day, he heard that this man Jesus was coming into the village of Jericho. Zacchaeus wanted to see Jesus pass by, so he ran to a blossoming fig tree, climbed up, and sat and watched Jesus approaching.

Suddenly, Jesus stopped at the very tree Zacchaeus had climbed up and called, "Zacchaeus, hurry on down, for I must stay at your house today!"[44]

Zacchaeus was overjoyed that Jesus wanted to fellowship with him and joyfully welcomed Jesus into his home. This changed his life forever. He repented, and his destiny was sealed for eternity.

Jesus declared that His main business was to seek out and give life to those who are lost.[45] That wasn't what most of His business associates ever believed was an acceptable way to do business in the marketplace—not his family, friends, religious leaders, or government officials. Jesus became ridiculed and criticized and eventually severely threatened to death. In the end, Jesus did indeed end up sacrificing His life so that the whole world would be saved and ultimately have eternal life with Him, the Savior of the World.

Because Jesus's mission was always about the eternal and never about the temporary, even the worst sinners were radically changed into generous disciples and wise Kingdom investors. He changed corrupt thieves into generous givers. In fact, Zacchaeus the tax collector told Jesus, "Half of all that I own I will give to the poor. And Lord, if I have cheated anyone, I promise to pay them back four times as much as I stole."[46] No one is beyond redemption. Because of Jesus, today you and everyone else can have a business done God's way that flourishes, where multitudes of people will start living abundantly and eternally. The influence of this little man's big witness changed the world around him, and God wants to do it again and again for you and me.

Ask yourself this: What am I doing to develop extraordinary generosity with an eternally focused heart and mind?

FIVE

The Great Commandment

Love the Lord your God with every passion of
your heart, with all the energy of your being,
and with every thought that is within you. This
is the great and supreme commandment. And the
second is like it in importance: You must love
your friend in the same way you love yourself.
Matthew 22:37–39

The Great Commission

Now wherever you go, make disciples of all
nations, baptizing them in the name of the
Father, the Son, and the Holy Spirit. And teach
them to faithfully follow all that I have
commanded you. And never forget that I am with
you every day, even to the completion of this age.
Matthew 28:19–20

MAKE A GREAT COMMITMENT TO GOD'S GREAT COMMANDMENT AND GOD'S GREAT COMMISSION

Matthew was chosen by Jesus to be one of His trusted disciples. A very wealthy and successful businessman, Matthew authored the book of Matthew in the Bible. In it, he recorded the Great Commandment and the Great Commission. Matthew learned these powerful principles directly from Jesus.

Words spoken directly from Jesus to someone in the Bible are referred to as "red-letter words" because most translations of the Bible print His words in red ink. The powerful words of Jesus regarding the Great Commandment (Matthew 22:37–39) and the Great Commission (Matthew 28:19–20) are the cornerstone for doing business God's way.

A truly great model for every business is to wholeheartedly and enthusiastically make a great commitment to the two key principles of doing business God's way: (1) the Great Commandment; and (2) the Great Commission. Modeling every business after two of the greatest life and business principles in the Bible is exceptionally wise and eternally profitable! This is God's perfect model for everyone to live a prosperous life and grow a business God's way, which is the only way to succeed in absolutely everything. The Great Commandment and the Great Commission were given to us by the most successful businessperson who ever walked the face of the Earth, Jesus, who was the ultimate model of how to live every day of our lives with eternity in our hearts and on our minds.

Jesus teaches both principles in the Bible. Let's reexamine the first one, briefly mentioned in chapter 3, the Great Commandment, which has two components to it. In Matthew, Jesus says, "LOVE THE LORD YOUR GOD WITH EVERY PASSION IN YOUR HEART, WITH ALL THE ENERGY OF YOUR BEING, AND WITH EVERY THOUGHT THAT IS WITHIN YOU. THIS IS THE GREAT AND SUPREME COMMANDMENT AND THE SECOND IS LIKE IT IN IMPORTANCE: 'YOU MUST LOVE YOUR FRIEND IN THE SAME WAY YOU LOVE YOURSELF.'"[47] These words contain the way to reach the pinnacle of building a lasting business God's way.

How do you apply this to your own business today? In order to apply it, you must grapple with the following questions and sincerely respond.

Application Questions

Ask yourself these questions: Are you loving your neighbor? Would your neighborhood, your city, your state, your country, or even the world you live in really miss your business if it closed down tomorrow? What difference does your business make in people's lives? In other words, who is impacted because of doing business with you?

> By loving God and loving people, you can transform an ordinary customer into an enthusiastic, raving fan.

Succeeding at business always involves more than a transactional exchange of money for goods and services. Every lasting marketplace is birthed through relationship; therefore, Epic Marketplace Revival must be relational first, just like Christ is relational with each of us. Our relationship with Christ influences our relationships with everyone else, whether personally or professionally. Products never outrank people. That's why Jesus said in the Great Commandment that we are to love Him and love your neighbor as yourself, but it is so much more than just your local community.

Jesus, the ultimate business initiator and sustainer, continuously emphasized another principle, the Great Commission. This principle is essential to building our businesses with never-ending success by going beyond ourselves and our business and joining God's vision and mission for the *global* Epic Marketplace Revival.

Jesus spoke these words to His disciples, known as the Great Commission:

> ALL AUTHORITY OF THE UNIVERSE HAS BEEN GIVEN TO ME. NOW WHEREVER YOU GO, MAKE DISCIPLES OF ALL NATIONS, BAPTIZING THEM IN THE NAME OF THE FATHER, THE SON, AND THE HOLY SPIRIT. AND TEACH THEM TO FAITH-FULLY FOLLOW ALL THAT I HAVE COMMANDED YOU. AND NEVER FORGET THAT I AM WITH YOU EVERY DAY, EVEN TO THE COMPLETION OF THIS AGE.[48]

Jesus expands on the Great Commandment, of loving your neighbor, when He commissions His people to go into the nations and create a global revival. An Epic Marketplace Revival is created by a ripple effect, and by multiplication. In practical application, my friend Ken Blanchard always told me that success comes from building loyalty-committed customers, called "raving fans." He explained that raving fans will stay lined up by the way you conduct business as you *genuinely* and *lovingly* exceed their expectations. By loving God and loving people, you can transform an ordinary customer into an enthusiastic, raving fan.

God tells us that living as His disciples requires more than being a casual provider of goods and services. Customers are not often fully devoted until they become

B - Break
O - Out
O - Of
M - Mediocrity

a disciple of your company's goods and services. At that point, they become your greatest advertisers and advocates—eager, ready, willing, and waiting to do business with you. As a business owner or executive for top-performing employees, your goal is to turn every possible person into a disciple who shares your vision and your values, not only by what they say, but by how they live. This demonstrates living proof to the people around them that your business is the only business to do business with! Where the customer is impacted mentally, emotionally, physically, and spiritually, not only will your business experience healthy growth, but God's purpose and passion for your business to win the lost and lead them to an abundant and eternal life, will flourish.

My wife and I have worked with business coaches Larry and Staci Wallace, Fueled by Fire, who always emphasize how important B.O.O.M. is to the success of doing business God's way. This acronym stands for "Breaking Out of Mediocrity." When your business and God's business are united with God's morals, values, and ethics, there will be a big B.O.O.M. that will cause your business to "Break Out of Mediocrity." It is those essential principles that will become the catalyst for igniting clarity, alignment, and sustained momentum to do business God's way.

B.O.O.M. Essentials

The following eight steps are critical to B.O.O.M.:

1. Refuel with the daily reading of God's manual, the Bible, for best business practices. God says in Joshua 1:8, "Contemplate it day and night and be careful to follow every word it contains; then you will enjoy incredible prosperity and success."
2. Love one another.
3. Be obedient to God's way-of-doing-business blueprints.
4. Relentlessly pursue truth.
5. Offer exceptional, sacrificial service.
6. Model genuine humility.
7. Become really good at extending mercy and forgiveness.
8. Pray nonstop blessings for each employee, customer, vendor, owner, and coworker.

The Word of God does the work of God. The Bible is jam packed with God's wisdom. These God-given, essential steps will grow every business that practices them! God's power and promises will be unleashed beyond what anyone could possibly dream or imagine possible! In fact, God Himself assures us, "No eye has seen, no ear has heard, and no mind has imagined what God has prepared for those who love him."[49]

I have learned more successful business operating procedures, principles, and practices from the Bible than any other business manual, seminar, podcast, or other media presentation that I have ever seen. The Bible is packed with solid business successes in every one of the sixty-six books!

> **The Word of God does the work of God.**

An example of this is the book of Ephesians, where a very successful businessman, whose name was Paul, wrote standard operating procedures for everyone who is an employer or will be employed. God's instructions can be trusted to help us become wildly successful in every arena of life, especially in navigating an Epic Marketplace Revival. Always chase after God's instructions with great diligence and determination.

You who are team leaders or those who have management responsibilities also have an obligation to instruct your team members to wholeheartedly chase after God's instructions with great diligence and determination. You also have a mandate from God to serve your employees with humility in your heart, as though you were working for Jesus, the Master! You are the example for all those around you.

This stewardship as an employer requires teaching your employees to act with love and grace to one another, serving one another. Teaching them to always do what is right, even if others are not watching, so they may please Christ as His servants by doing His will. His way. Be assured that anything that you do that is beautiful and excellent will be repaid by your Lord. Make sure that you always do what is right, by forgiving those who offend you. Then you will know that there is a master in Heaven that shows no favoritism.

There's a story of the little boy who loved to play Monopoly with his grandmother. They would play their hearts out to gain as many properties and as much money as they could. The little boy could never beat his grandmother, until that one fateful day. He did it! He finally beat his grandmother. He was so proud, and he did not want the feeling or the game to end.

> We have one life to live, it will soon be passed; only what's done for Christ will last.

However, his grandmother had one more lesson for him to learn that day. The most important life lesson his grandmother taught him, and most memorable, was not about who won or who lost. The big, audacious lesson he learned was that at the end of the Monopoly game, all the game pieces, including property and money, *go back in the box.*

When our lives on Earth are over, all the material things that we value so much go back in the box. As I reflect on this story, it reminds me of the childhood lesson I mentioned in chapter 1, that I learned from my dad, "We have one life to live, it will soon be passed; only what's done for Christ will last."

God's way of doing both life and business is to love God with everything we have! Next is to love God's people in the same way we love ourselves. Following that commandment, God commissions us with the authority to go everywhere we can and do everything we can to make disciples. When those disciples are filled with white-hot passion to make more disciples, this cycle continues until everyone everywhere in the whole world is saved! Salvation is the permanent, most important, bottom line of life and business that ultimately will lead to a global marketplace revival. This will bring uncontainable joy to God's heart along with joy to the world!

Ask yourself this: Am I totally committed to God's Great Commandment and God's Great Commission?

SIX

Yahweh, you're the bedrock beneath my feet,
my faith-fortress, my wonderful deliverer, my God,
my rock of rescue where none can reach me.
You're the shield around me, the mighty power
that saves me, and my high place.
Psalm 18:2

HOW TO BUILD A ROCK-SOLID BUSINESS THAT WILL LAST FOREVER!

During my lifetime, as I built my own homes, as well as schools, businesses, places of worship, and other structures, I placed a Bible in every foundation as a reminder that the solid rock of Jesus Christ is the very foundation of all that we build. All other ground is sinking sand! There was nothing magical that took place. However, there was something powerful!

Honoring God as the rock-solid foundation is a matter of faith and trust. Building a rock-solid foundation is not only necessary for constructing a physical structure but also essential for building your life and business. What foundation have you built for your business? Your life? Your family? Your finances? It does matter. It matters tremendously!

Building on the Rock

In the book of Matthew, Jesus emphasized the importance of building our life's unshakable foundation when He said the following:

EVERYONE WHO HEARS MY TEACHING AND APPLIES IT TO HIS LIFE CAN BE COMPARED TO A WISE MAN WHO BUILT HIS HOUSE ON AN UNSHAKABLE FOUNDATION. WHEN THE RAINS FELL AND THE FLOOD CAME, WITH FIERCE WINDS BEATING UPON HIS HOUSE, IT STOOD FIRM BECAUSE OF ITS STRONG FOUNDATION. BUT EVERYONE WHO HEARS MY TEACHING AND DOES NOT APPLY IT TO HIS LIFE CAN BE COMPARED TO A FOOLISH MAN WHO BUILT HIS HOUSE ON THE SAND. WHEN IT RAINED AND RAINED AND THE FLOOD CAME, WITH WIND AND WAVES BEATING UPON HIS HOUSE, IT COLLAPSED AND WAS SWEPT AWAY.[50]

It's a fact that in every area of life, the words of Jesus are effective and powerful. There are numerous Bible verses that

> **Want your business to last forever? Build it God's way!**

declare the truth about building a solid foundation on God's principles. These are extremely helpful as you work together with your business partners, associates, friends, family, neighbors, customers, and vendors.

Another great verse with a rock-solid promise is written in 1 Corinthians 3:11: "For no one is empowered to lay an alternative foundation other than the good foundation that exists, which is Jesus Christ!" The author continues in verses 12–15 to tell us what happens when we build upon this foundation:

> The quality of materials used by anyone building on this foundation will soon be made apparent, whether it has been built with gold, silver, and costly stones, or wood, hay, and straw. Their work will soon become evident, for the Day will make it clear, because it will be revealed by blazing fire! And the fire will test and prove the workmanship of each builder. If his work stands the test of fire, he will be rewarded. If his work is consumed by the fire, he will suffer great loss. Yet he himself will barely escape destruction, like one being rescued out of a burning house.

The reality is that if we try to carry out God's mission and vision without Jesus, our firm foundation, it will inevitably crumble. The future storms that disrupt everyone's life, relationships, businesses, and faith will be destructive without a solid foundation underneath you! How we build our businesses matters to God!

Fruitful Alignment

If we want our businesses to outlive us and receive eternal benefits and rewards, we need to do business God's way. The Bible confirms this when Jesus tells us:

> SO YOU MUST REMAIN IN LIFE-UNION WITH ME, FOR I REMAIN IN LIFE-UNION WITH YOU. FOR AS A BRANCH SEVERED FROM THE VINE WILL NOT BEAR FRUIT, SO YOUR LIFE WILL BE FRUIT-LESS UNLESS YOU LIVE YOUR LIFE INTIMATELY JOINED TO MINE. I AM THE SPROUTING VINE AND YOU'RE MY BRANCHES. AS YOU LIVE IN UNION WITH ME AS YOUR SOURCE, FRUITFUL-NESS WILL STREAM FROM WITHIN YOU—BUT WHEN YOU LIVE SEPARATED FROM ME YOU ARE POWERLESS. IF A PERSON IS SEPARATED FROM ME, HE IS DISCARDED; SUCH BRANCHES ARE GATHERED UP AND THROWN INTO THE FIRE TO BE BURNED. BUT IF YOU LIVE IN LIFE-UNION WITH ME AND IF MY WORDS LIVE POWERFULLY WITHIN YOU—THEN YOU CAN ASK WHATEVER YOU DESIRE AND IT WILL BE DONE. WHEN YOUR LIVES BEAR ABUNDANT FRUIT, YOU DEMONSTRATE THAT YOU ARE MY MATURE DISCIPLES WHO GLORIFY MY FATHER![51]

No one can fulfill God's present, eternal plans or purposes without His power and His presence.

God's vision is possible because He is the victorious visionary. With God in charge, we are compelled to celebrate every vision and victory by giving God the credit for all the success that happened in business and in life. It becomes an uncontainable celebration as we let everyone know that our

> **When God wins, He makes sure everyone around Him feels His pleasure.**

great God showed up and pulled off a vision that never could have been accomplished without Him. When God wins, He makes sure everyone around Him feels His pleasure. Yes! His pleasure feels so good.

Values That Endure

An important foundational piece of establishing our businesses requires that we lay the foundation with values that honor God.

What does God value most?

Unquestionably, God values people more than policies, procedures, profits, or possessions. He tells us in Genesis, the very first book of the Bible, that we are made in His image. We are the face and voice and hands and feet and heart and mind of God. So the values of our businesses need to reflect how valuable people are to God and to us.

In Matthew 23:11–12, Jesus tells us how critical the value of humility is, in conducting not only our businesses, but also our lives:

THE GREATEST AMONG YOU WILL BE THE ONE WHO ALWAYS SERVES OTHERS. REMEMBER THIS: IF YOU HAVE A LOFTY OPINION OF YOURSELF AND SEEK TO BE HONORED, YOU WILL BE HUMBLED. BUT IF YOU HAVE A MODEST OPINION OF YOURSELF AND CHOOSE TO HUMBLE YOURSELF, YOU WILL BE HONORED.

If anyone wants to be great, they must be a servant of every person who crosses their path. Humility is self-lessness and being servant-minded. It is having a healthy self-esteem, not a prideful or self-important one.[52] It is other-focused instead of self-focused.

Additionally, God greatly values "grace-full-ness." Being full of grace and extending grace in the same way that we have been given grace pleases God! It is only by grace, through faith, that it is possible for anyone to be successful.

Two more essential values important to God are kindness and forgiveness. In Ephesians 4:30-32, Paul speaks of being kind and forgiving to one another in the same way God has lavished His kindness and forgiveness upon you and me.

So never grieve the Spirit of God or take for granted his holy influence in your life. Lay aside bitter words, temper tantrums, revenge, profanity, and insults. But instead be kind and affectionate toward one another. Has God graciously forgiven you? Then graciously forgive one another in the depths of Christ's love.

Leadership Worth Following

In Ephesians 5:1, God said for us to be imitators of Him in everything we do because then we can represent

> Always live in the truth and keep your promises.

our Father well as beloved sons and daughters. Christ calls us to walk surrendered to Him and consistently and constantly show extravagant love. Such extravagant love is pleasing to God because Christ's extravagant love through His extravagant sacrifice was first shown to us. Christ's "great love for us was pleasing to God, like an aroma of adoration—a sweet healing fragrance."[53] Therefore, fellow travelers on this journey to glorify God and "do business God's way," continue to walk surrendered, demonstrating the extravagant love of Christ so that we, too, may be pleasing to God like an aroma of adoration, a sweet-smelling fragrance.

Inherent within all these values is truth telling. The wisdom of Proverbs, which is one of my favorite books in the Bible, gives us guidance from the wisest man of his day and time. King Solomon said, "Truthfulness marks the righteous, but the habitual liar can never be trusted. . . . Truthful words will stand the test of time, but one day every lie will be seen for what it is. . . . Live in the truth and keep your promises, and the Lord will keep delighting in you, but he detests a liar."[54] Living and speaking the truth is one of God's greatest commandments.

Godly Virtues

Yet another rock to build God's business upon is godly virtues. Peter, who Jesus named "The Rock," shares in one of his letters everything we need for a virtuous and godly life.[55] When we allow God to be in charge of our businesses, He invites us to participate in the magnificent rewards of virtuous pursuits. God calls you and me to devote ourselves to lavishly expressing our faith with goodness and understanding. We are told by God to devote ourselves to understanding the strength of self-control, but self-control by itself is insufficient. We must also experience patient endurance. Building from patient endurance, we must produce godliness. But it does not stop there. The results of godliness will be mercy toward our brothers and sisters. All of these culminate in giving others what Christ has extended to us—unending love!

When these virtues are already planted deep within us, the Bible assures us that Christ has been put in charge. When we possess these values in abundant supply, God guarantees us that they will keep us from being inactive or fruitless in our pursuit of knowing Jesus Christ more intimately. God clearly points out that if anyone lacks these things, they are constantly closing their eyes to the treasures of our faith.

For this reason, beloved ones, be eager to confirm and validate that God has invited you to salvation and claimed you as his own. If you do these things, you will never stumble. As a result, the kingdom's gates will open wide to you as God choreographs your triumphant entrance into the eternal kingdom of our Lord and Savior, Jesus the Messiah.[56]

Incredible!

Still another essential virtue is a God-honoring vocabulary. Building a God-honoring vocabulary that is spoken in your business may be continuously challenging to instill, yet it is rewarding! A life-giving, God-honoring vocabulary for all staff, customers, vendors, and other business contacts will bless every business. The Bible tells us that our wise words are like deep waters that spring forth from within, bubbling up inside the one with understanding. God tells us that words are so powerful they can kill or give new life.[57] What we say reveals what's truly in our hearts. Our language and our vocabulary really matter to God! Jesus taught us very clearly about a vocabulary that will honor him and establish a healthy, eternal foundation.

> **Words give life—or destroys it.**

Then Jesus turned to the crowd and said, "COME, LISTEN AND OPEN YOUR HEART TO UNDERSTAND. WHAT TRULY CONTAMINATES

A PERSON IS NOT WHAT HE PUTS INTO HIS MOUTH BUT WHAT COMES OUT OF HIS MOUTH. THAT'S WHAT MAKES PEOPLE DEFILED."

Then his disciples approached him, and said, "Don't you know that what you just said offended the Pharisees?[58]

In other words, Pharisees are the type of people who couldn't care less about their language and vocabularies.

Jesus replied, "EVERY PLANT THAT MY HEAVENLY FATHER DIDN'T PLANT IS DESTINED TO BE UPROOTED. STAY AWAY FROM THEM, FOR THEY'RE NOTHING MORE THAN BLIND GUIDES. DO YOU KNOW WHAT HAPPENS WHEN A BLIND MAN PRETENDS TO GUIDE ANOTHER BLIND MAN? THEY BOTH STUMBLE INTO A DITCH!"[59]

"IS IT HARD TO UNDERSTAND THAT WHATEVER YOU EAT ENTERS THE STOMACH ONLY TO PASS OUT INTO THE SEWER? BUT WHAT COMES OUT OF YOUR MOUTH REVEALS THE CORE OF YOUR HEART. WORDS CAN POLLUTE, NOT FOOD. YOU WILL FIND LIVING WITHIN AN IMPURE HEART EVIL IDEAS, MURDEROUS THOUGHTS, ADULTERY, SEXUAL IMMORALITY,

THEFT, LIES, AND SLANDER. THAT'S WHAT
POLLUTES A PERSON."[60]

Jesus's reference to Pharisees highlights those who dis-regard language and vocabulary—and the effect it has on others. But it is so important. In fact, it's paramount in every business to have God-sized standards for expressing words that produce life into one another, and to clarify the words that destroy life.

Culture That Speaks Life

Last, but not least, is the virtue of vitality. Vitality is another word for enthusiasm. We already discussed that in Greek, *enthusiasm* means "being full of God." Enthusiasm is extremely contagious. An enthusiastic vocabulary pro-duces enthusiastic attitudes and actions. Many businesses we walk into have a sense of great joy. Other businesses we walk into have a sense of joyless-

> **Enthusiasm is extremely contagious.**

ness. One of the sure signs of a company committed to building eternal foundations are the ones that are overflowing with joyfulness. God tells us that His joy is the source of our strength!

My wife and I begin every day, before our feet hit the floor, with the following declaration: "This is the day that the Lord has made! We are going to rejoice and be glad in it." No matter what's happening, my wife and I have determined to choose Jesus-sized joy as our foundation to launch into building a skyscraper day!

Ask yourself this: Have I chosen Jesus Christ to be the foundation of my life, my family, and my business?

SEVEN

And show hospitality to strangers,
for they may be angels from God showing
up as your guests.
Hebrews 13:2

BUSINESSES THAT ARE BUILT TO LAST EXCEL AT EXCEPTIONAL HOSPITALITY

Some years ago, when I was speaking in Hawaii, a minister's wife shared with me a true story of what happened to her family one Thanksgiving Day.

On Thanksgiving Day, she went to her refrigerator to look for some food to fix for her children for their Thanksgiving meal. She discovered that there were only two hotdogs left to eat. Even though there wasn't much food, she decided to make their Thanksgiving celebration memorable by going to the beach and building a fire in a pit where her two children could toast their hot dogs on a stick! She said that they all had a lot of fun together, but they were all still very hungry.

As they headed back to their apartment, a lady shouted out to them, asking if they were hungry. They all admitted that they were very hungry. She then invited them to come inside her apartment to eat a Thanksgiving meal with her. The mom followed the two children as they ran up three flights of stairs to join this wonderful lady and share a delicious meal! They all laughed together and ate as much as they possibly could fit in; they even ended up taking containers of leftover food home with them. They all hugged goodbye and headed home.

> "I get to serve" changes the room. "I have to serve" drains it.

Three days later, they went back to return the food containers that were sent home with them and to give the hospitable lady a heartfelt, handwritten thank-you note. They knocked on the door to the apartment where they had all enjoyed their delicious Thanksgiving meal together. However, there was no answer. As they continued knocking at the door, the manager of the apartments happened to walk by and saw them knocking. She informed them that no one lived in that apartment. In fact, the apartment had been vacant for several months. At that moment, the realization sunk in that they had spent Thanksgiving Day with an angel sent by God. Wow! You may have heard the phrase, "I don't care how much you know, until I know how much you care." Positive speaking with a hospitality attitude and heart looks more like, "I get to serve you," instead of "I have to serve you." Or "I get to help you," instead of "I have to help you."

The "Get To" Mindset

Whether we are talking to strangers, friends, customers, members of our family, or people who live in our neighborhood, "WE GET TO" helps us live out authentic hospitality that exudes and creates a friendly environment. Someone once said to me, "Who knows when we may be extending hospitality to an angel?" If we picture each person we encounter at work or at home as someone sent by God, we may find ourselves crossing paths with an angel each day. How would we treat them? God may sometimes send His Heavenly angelic hosts to test us and our willingness to express kindness and unconditional, nonjudgmental love to those around us.

Jesus often spoke in parables, which were simple stories used to illustrate a moral lesson. In Luke, we read one of the great parables Jesus told. It was the story of the good Samaritan.

Jesus replied, "THERE WAS ONCE A JEWISH MAN TRAVELING FROM JERUSALEM TO JERICHO WHEN BANDITS ROBBED HIM ALONG THE WAY. THEY BEAT HIM SEVERELY, STRIPPED HIM NAKED, AND LEFT HIM HALF DEAD.

SOON, A JEWISH PRIEST WALKING DOWN THE SAME ROAD CAME UPON THE WOUNDED MAN. SEEING HIM FROM A DISTANCE, THE PRIEST CROSSED TO THE OTHER SIDE OF THE

ROAD AND WALKED RIGHT PAST HIM, NOT
TURNING TO HELP HIM ONE BIT.

LATER, A RELIGIOUS MAN, A LEVITE, CAME
WALKING DOWN THE SAME ROAD AND LIKE-
WISE CROSSED TO THE OTHER SIDE TO PASS BY
THE WOUNDED MAN WITHOUT STOPPING TO
HELP HIM.

FINALLY, ANOTHER MAN, A SAMARITAN,
CAME UPON THE BLEEDING MAN AND WAS
MOVED WITH TENDER COMPASSION FOR HIM.
HE STOOPED DOWN AND GAVE HIM FIRST AID,
POURING OLIVE OIL ON HIS WOUNDS, DISIN-
FECTING THEM WITH WINE, AND BANDAGING
THEM TO STOP THE BLEEDING. LIFTING HIM
UP, HE PLACED HIM ON HIS OWN DONKEY AND
BROUGHT HIM TO AN INN. THEN HE TOOK
HIM FROM HIS DONKEY AND CARRIED HIM TO
A ROOM FOR THE NIGHT. THE NEXT MORNING
HE TOOK HIS OWN MONEY FROM HIS WALLET
AND GAVE IT TO THE INNKEEPER WITH THESE
WORDS: 'TAKE CARE OF HIM UNTIL I COME
BACK FROM MY JOURNEY. IF IT COSTS MORE
THAN THIS, I WILL REPAY YOU WHEN I RETURN.'
SO, NOW, TELL ME, WHICH ONE OF THE THREE
MEN WHO SAW THE WOUNDED MAN PROVED
TO BE THE TRUE NEIGHBOR?"

The religious scholar responded, "The one who
demonstrated kindness and mercy."

Jesus said, "GO AND DO THE SAME AS HE."[61]

I love this story! It points out that the Good Samaritan saw an opportunity to "GET TO" rather than "have to," express heaven-like hospitality. No matter what our demanding schedule may be, to love as Jesus loved and do what Jesus did expresses to the world what it's like to always live as Jesus lived.

Daily, Jesus stoops down to touch us, help us, and heal us. Jesus lifts us up and carries us along our journey, and He promises to reward those who do this for others. As we seek to build a business that lasts and make disciples instead of simply making money, we want to not only speak about Christ's love for us but also express it in our actions.

Immeasurable Hospitality

Jesus gave us another illustration of exceptional hospitality in Luke 10 beginning with verse 38.

As Jesus and the disciples continued on their journey, they came to a village where a woman welcomed Jesus into her home. Her name was Martha, and she had a sister named Mary. Mary sat down attentively before the Master, absorbing every revelation he shared. But Martha became exasperated with finishing the numerous household chores in preparation for her guests, so she interrupted Jesus and said, "Lord, don't you think it's unfair that my sister left me to do all the work by myself? You should tell her to get up and help me."

The Lord answered her, "MARTHA, MY BELOVED MARTHA. WHY ARE YOU UPSET AND TROUBLED, PULLED AWAY BY ALL THESE MANY DISTRACTIONS? MARY HAS DISCOVERED THE ONE THING MOST IMPORTANT BY CHOOSING TO SIT AT MY FEET. SHE IS UNDISTRACTED, AND I WON'T TAKE THIS PRIVILEGE FROM HER."[62]

What a great picture of immeasurable hospitality!

Few leaders understand that hospitality begins with presence, not performance. When Jesus responded to Martha, it was not out of *rebuke* but *reorientation*. True hospitality isn't just about what you prepare—it's about being fully present with the one before you.

In a legacy-driven company, the most enduring hospitality creates an environment where people are seen, heard, and spiritually nourished. It's the difference between transactional care and relational connection. Mary's posture reminds us that immeasurable hospitality isn't measured by output—it's measure by heart.

Jesus sacrificed everything for us so that we would experience what it's like to be accepted and unconditionally loved. We are commanded by God to treat all people as though we were God's personal ambassadors, representing God Himself. Let your business be a place where people don't just feel served—they feel significant. That's leadership rooted in Heaven's blueprint.

Who wouldn't want to do business with a company that had the heart of our loving Heavenly Father?

A modern-day example of this is the well-known company Chick-fil-A. Whenever you ask for something whether your food is too cold or you need something else, they always say, "It's my pleasure." If we could have an "it's my pleasure" attitude, the marketplace would be an attractively welcoming place. It's my pleasure to

> **Let your business be a place where people don't just feel served— they feel significant.**

serve you. It's my pleasure to encourage you. It's my pleasure to help you in every way that I possibly can. If we lead by example, it will indeed ignite an Epic Marketplace Revival that would greatly please our Heavenly Father and help change marketplace attitudes and perspectives, so that every business can be totally aligned with doing business God's way. God-like hospitality would not only be attractive for everyone looking to do business with each of us, but ultimately produce unprecedented profitability in every arena of life as well as business.

WHEN THE SON OF MAN APPEARS IN HIS MAJESTIC GLORY, WITH ALL HIS ANGELS BY HIS SIDE, HE WILL TAKE HIS SEAT ON HIS THRONE OF SPLENDOR, AND ALL THE NATIONS

WILL BE GATHERED TOGETHER BEFORE HIM. AND LIKE A SHEPHERD WHO SEPARATES THE SHEEP FROM THE GOATS, HE WILL SEPARATE ALL THE PEOPLE. THE "SHEEP" HE WILL PUT ON HIS RIGHT SIDE AND THE "GOATS" ON HIS LEFT. THEN THE KING WILL TURN TO THOSE ON HIS RIGHT AND SAY, "YOU HAVE A SPECIAL PLACE IN MY FATHER'S HEART. COME AND EXPERIENCE THE FULL INHERITANCE OF THE KINGDOM REALM THAT HAS BEEN DESTINED FOR YOU FROM BEFORE THE FOUNDATION OF THE WORLD! FOR WHEN YOU SAW ME HUNGRY, YOU FED ME. WHEN YOU FOUND ME THIRSTY, YOU GAVE ME DRINK. WHEN I HAD NO PLACE TO STAY, YOU INVITED ME IN, AND WHEN I WAS POORLY CLOTHED, YOU COVERED ME. WHEN I WAS SICK, YOU TENDERLY CARED FOR ME, AND WHEN I WAS IN PRISON YOU VISITED ME."

THEN THE GODLY WILL ANSWER HIM, "LORD, WHEN DID WE SEE YOU HUNGRY OR THIRSTY AND GIVE YOU FOOD AND SOMETHING TO DRINK? WHEN DID WE SEE YOU WITH NO PLACE TO STAY AND INVITE YOU IN? WHEN DID WE SEE YOU POORLY CLOTHED AND COVER YOU? WHEN DID WE SEE YOU SICK AND TENDERLY CARE FOR YOU, OR IN PRISON AND VISIT YOU?"

AND THE KING WILL ANSWER THEM, "DON'T YOU KNOW? WHEN YOU CARED FOR ONE OF THE LEAST OF THESE, MY LITTLE ONES, MY TRUE BROTHERS AND SISTERS, YOU DEMONSTRATED LOVE FOR ME."[63]

The business lesson we learn from what Jesus taught is that as we are hospitable, as we love and serve and help others, we are actually helping Jesus. When all our staff and employees, customers and vendors, and all our marketplace partners understand the true meaning of doing business God's way, God's resources will supply, encourage, and inspire each employee and employer along with the owner. How very pleased God is when everyone is willing to represent Jesus Christ, as Lord over their business.

The Ultimate Servant's Heart

Another powerful story from God's manual of doing business God's way is where Jesus Himself washes the feet of His disciples. It is the ultimate example of true humility and servant leadership.

Now Jesus was fully aware that the Father had placed all things under his control, for he had come from God and was about to go back to be with him. So he got up from the meal and took off his outer robe, and took a towel and wrapped it around his waist. Then he poured water into a basin and began to wash the disciples' dirty feet and dry them with his towel.

But when Jesus got to Simon Peter, he objected and said, "I can't let you wash my dirty feet—you're my Lord!"

Jesus replied, "You don't understand yet the meaning of what I'm doing, but soon it will be clear to you."

Peter looked at Jesus and said, "You'll never wash my dirty feet—never!"

"But Peter, if you don't allow me to wash your feet," Jesus responded, "then you will not be able to share life with me." So Peter said, "Lord, in that case, don't just wash my feet, wash my hands and my head too!"

Jesus said to him, "You are already clean. You've been washed completely and you just need your feet to be cleansed—but that can't be said of all of you." For Jesus knew which one was about to betray him, and that's why he told them that not all of them were clean.

After washing their feet, he put his robe on and returned to his place at the table. "Do you understand what I just did?" Jesus said.

"You've called me your teacher and Lord, and you're right, for that's who I am. So if I'm your teacher and Lord and

HAVE JUST WASHED YOUR DIRTY FEET, THEN YOU SHOULD FOLLOW THE EXAMPLE THAT I'VE SET FOR YOU AND WASH ONE ANOTHER'S DIRTY FEET. NOW DO FOR EACH OTHER WHAT I HAVE JUST DONE FOR YOU. I SPEAK TO YOU TIMELESS TRUTH: A SERVANT IS NOT SUPERIOR TO HIS MASTER, AND AN APOSTLE IS NEVER GREATER THAN THE ONE WHO SENT HIM. SO NOW PUT INTO PRACTICE WHAT I HAVE DONE FOR YOU, AND YOU WILL EXPERIENCE A LIFE OF HAPPINESS ENRICHED WITH UNTOLD BLESSINGS!"[64]

If we will truly embrace this story, it holds the power to shape not only what we believe—but how we live, lead, and engage in the marketplace. When its truth takes root in us, it compels Kingdom-minded action in our business practices. It challenges us to stay humble and servant minded. It becomes not only a place where we as Christ followers can be a light for Christ, but it becomes a place where people are discipled. It becomes a place where lives are transformed for eternity. That, my friends, is the bottom line of building a business that truly lasts. If you build a business that consistently operates God's way, you will experience a life filled with uncontainable joy and uncontainable blessings day after day after day. Who wouldn't want to be doing business or working for a business like that? In the marketplace today, people are yearning for simple hospitality gestures. These are powerful expressions that Jesus Christ modeled for His faithful followers.

Years ago, I saw firsthand Jesus's servant-heart attitude put into action by the former CEO of Chick-fil-A, Dan Cathy. A small group of us were at a meeting in Chicago with Dan when he brought out several shoeshine brushes. As the small group of business leaders were sitting around a conference table, he dropped to his knees and humbly shined each person's shoes. This was an unforgettable, humble expression of what was truly in his heart. His heart overflowed with a servant's hospitality and a contagious "shoeshine attitude."

Servant Leadership Works

Jesus told us that if we want to be truly great, we need to develop the heart of a servant. God calls every person to live as a humble servant always. Business is never just about making money. If our business is to succeed, we must wholeheartedly commit to being hospitable, humble servants of all. The Epic Marketplace Revival will set the benchmark on how to build a hospitable business that is focused on eternity.

Jesus's mighty expressions of hospitality are:

1. Be positive, especially around negative people.
2. Be encouraging to others, especially around those who are discouraged.

3. Be truthful, especially around those who tend to not be truthful.
4. Be kind, especially to those who are rude.
5. Be available to serve, especially to those who are struggling and confused.
6. Be complimentary, especially around those who are hurting.
7. Be courteous, especially around those who are inconsiderate and self-seeking.
8. Be joyful, especially around those who are joyless.
9. Be forgiving, especially around those who are holding onto unforgiveness.
10. Be a great listener, especially to those who are yearning to be heard.
11. Be generous, especially around those who are selfish.
12. Be loving with unconditional, nonjudgmental love, especially to those who are unlovable.

Prayer: The Heartbeat of Hospitality

One of the best, most influential ways to be hospitable is to pray with and for one another. Prayer can be done silently or spoken aloud. Praying for each guest, each customer, each person that we get to help and serve and do business with will change everything. Prayer works wonders.

God greatly honors, and delights in, those who are *ALL IN* and *ALL OUT* for Jesus—the Savior of the world.

They will be powerful instruments in the hands of God, to pour out His uncontainable blessings.

When we are blessed, we are called to be a blessing. I have personally found that the greatest way to bless another person is to pray for them and simply share a heartfelt smile that will fill them with peace and joy.

Every act of humility—every shoe shined, every hand lifted, every prayer whispered—is a seed sown into eternity. And when we choose to "get to" serve rather than "have to," we join Heaven's blueprint for lasting impact. Let your company reflect the heart of the Father, and you won't just attract customers—you'll activate transformation. Revival in the marketplace begins where servant-hearted hospitality starts. Try it! And you'll be amazed what God does!

Ask yourself this: Do I excel in exceptional hospitality?

EIGHT

Now faith brings our hopes into reality and becomes the foundation needed to acquire the things we long for. It is all the evidence required to prove what is still unseen.

Hebrews 11:1

THE EVERLASTING POWER OF BOLD FAITH

One Sunday afternoon, I got a phone call that my friend Don, who owned twenty-five McDonald's stores, had a heart attack and was in the emergency room at St. Joe's Hospital. I debated whether or not to go see Don, because I was exhausted from speaking at four church services that morning.

As I sat in my chair relaxing, God kept nudging me to go see Don and tell him that God wanted to give him a new heart. I thought, "What if I go and tell Don that You want to give him a new heart and he dies?" However, with bold faith I went to the hospital and told my friend that we needed to pray and trust that God would give him a new heart and that he was going to be strong and healthy with his new heart.

Obedience Unblocks Divine Favor

The next morning, Don called me with stunning news: The doctor told him that his sixty-nine-year-old heart looked brand-new—like that of a healthy twenty-year-old. Wow! A miracle had unfolded, and I had the privilege of witnessing it firsthand. By simply doing what God asked—visiting Don, praying with him, and believing that God would fulfill His promise—I saw bold faith activate divine healing in real time.

Faith Produces the Rocket Fuel for Revival

Faith is the powerful rocket fuel that creates and sustains great businesses! Faith affirms that anything is possible.

Another one of my personal experiences with miraculous faith came rushing into my life while I sat listening to a man of great faith, Dr. Robert Schuller, at a pastors' conference almost fifty

> **Mustard seed faith can move mountains.**

years ago. He said that faith is more than simply good news; rather faith is the rocket fuel of abundant and eternal life. He went on to say, faith brings our hopes into reality and becomes the foundation needed to acquire the things we long for. It provides the wisdom required to prove what is still unseen; faith empowers us to see that the universe was created and beautifully coordinated by the power of God's words. Without faith living within us, it would be impossible to please God.

The conference was interrupted with an urgent announcement, calling me out of the meeting regarding an accident with my three-year-old son, Patrick. I quickly learned that he was found at the bottom of the pool of the place where we were staying.

Dr. Schuller pulled me aside and asked me if I believed in the miracle of faith.

I said, "Yes."

We prayed, and I left to go to the hospital. Unbeknownst to me, while I was enroute to my son and family, there were over three hundred pastors at the conference who stopped the session to pray for a miracle.

When I reached the hospital, the doctor came out and said they could not find any water in Patrick's lungs, and he was crying for his mother and father. God not only performed a miracle that day, but God also showed Himself mightily to me regarding bold faith!

Dr. Robert Schuller was a man of faith and many positive words. He often encouraged me by telling me, "When faced with a mountain, do not quit. Make sure that you keep on striving until you either climb over, find a tunnel underneath, or simply stay in, and turn the mountain into a gold mine with God's help." We don't need a truckload of faith to successfully fulfill God's mission in the marketplace and live out God's call on our lives. No! God tells us we only need faith the size of a mustard seed.

Faith of A Mustard Seed—
Strategy That Works

Imagine in our marketplace business, doing business God's way, only needing a mustard seed. A mustard seed is one to two millimeters in diameter. Jesus promises us that's all the faith we need. A teeny, tiny bit! He is teaching us it's not about the size of our faith that is so powerful, rather, it is the immeasurable size of the power of the faith giver, God Himself. The Bible, our ultimate business manual, gives us our business operating principles.

In Matthew 17:20, it says that if you have faith inside of you no bigger than the size of a mustard seed, you can say to a mountain of trouble or problems or roadblocks, "Move away from here," or "Go over there," and you'll see the mountain move. The Bible tells us that there's nothing that we can't accomplish or overcome.[65]

I must admit that often in my own life I become so narrowly focused on the obstacle, the problem, or the mountain in front of me; instead of focusing on the mountain mover, who is Jesus Christ! His power unleashed within me causes mustard seed faith to be activated. So often I easily forget how to remove the mountain. Instead of going to God and telling Him how big my mountain is, I need to go to my mountain and tell it how big my God is.

This mountain-moving procedure of faith that Jesus continuously taught is described in Mark 11:23–26:

LISTEN TO THE TRUTH I SPEAK TO YOU: WHOEVER SAYS TO THIS MOUNTAIN WITH GREAT FAITH AND DOES NOT DOUBT, "MOUNTAIN, BE LIFTED UP AND THROWN INTO THE MIDST OF THE SEA," AND BELIEVES THAT WHAT HE SAYS WILL HAPPEN, IT WILL BE DONE. THIS IS THE REASON I URGE YOU TO BOLDLY BELIEVE FOR WHATEVER YOU ASK FOR IN PRAYER—BE CONVINCED THAT YOU HAVE RECEIVED IT AND IT WILL BE YOURS. AND WHENEVER YOU STAND PRAYING, IF YOU FIND THAT YOU CARRY SOMETHING IN YOUR HEART AGAINST ANOTHER PERSON, RELEASE HIM AND FORGIVE HIM SO THAT YOUR FATHER IN HEAVEN WILL ALSO RELEASE YOU AND FORGIVE YOU OF YOUR FAULTS. BUT IF YOU WILL NOT RELEASE FORGIVENESS, DON'T EXPECT YOUR FATHER IN HEAVEN TO RELEASE YOU FROM YOUR MISDEEDS.

Wow! Wouldn't marketplace business be so much more amazing if everyone conducted their life and business according to God's way? Faith fosters an atmosphere of trust, and trust fosters honesty. Honesty gives us the confident courage to take great leaps of faith, which would truly ignite an Epic Marketplace Revival!

Faith That Perseveres Beyond Profit

I have a friend who has a thriving law practice in Texas. My friend faced a significant business test. When his development project went bankrupt, all his partners in the development left vendors and financial institutions with unpaid debts. Nevertheless, my friend spent the next decade of his life making sure that everyone got paid. It was a very painful sacrifice; however, God rewarded him in unimaginable ways. Most importantly, my friend kept his honest, trustworthy reputation intact, which is more than all the silver and gold the world contains. Today, everyone wants to do business with him. When someone chooses to do business God's way, God always rewards them in ways that go beyond their greatest hopes and dreams. Working God's way, even though it may be the most difficult way, is forever worth it. Paul says, "Let us not become weary in doing good, for at the proper time we will reap a harvest if we do not give up."[66] God never promised that His way would be easy, yet He did promise that doing business His way would be worth it! Perseverance leads to blessings.

Moses Modeled Marketplace Morality

One of the most powerful and well-known faith stories in the Bible is about Moses—a mighty marketplace warrior who lived his life not just making a difference, but making a different world. In the wake of his leadership and total trust in God, God freed multitudes of abused slaves. Then God entrusted Moses with the standards for his nation, known as the Ten Commandments. When the nation obeyed the Ten Commandments, God ushered those citizens into a time of unprecedented prosperity. When they wholeheartedly sought after their relationship with God and obeyed these Commandments, they experienced God's favor on their families, their government, and their businesses.

The Ten Commandments can be found in Exodus 20:3–17 and are paraphrased as follows:

1. Worship only God.
   Put nothing else in His place.
2. Have no idols over God.
   Idols can be businesses, money, possessions, hobbies—anything that takes the place of God.
3. Do not use God's name in vain.
   Do not take God's name when swearing or cursing.
4. Keep the Sabbath day.
   Set aside one day a week for rest with no work. Focus your day on God. Hobby Lobby and Chick-fil-A are both closed on Sundays, and God has blessed those businesses abundantly.
5. Honor your father and mother.
   God says if you do this, you will experience long life.
6. Do not murder.

This commandment directly addresses physical murder. However, Jesus clearly says that words can either build someone up, or words can destroy them. This is also considered a murderous spirit.[67]

7. Do not commit adultery.
   Adultery is not just the act but also lusting after someone who is not your spouse. Be faithful in marriage—guard your heart and your covenant.

8. Do not steal.
   Walk in integrity and generosity.

9. Do not slander others.
   Slander is to bear false testimony or false witness against someone. This applies to other businesses and outside individuals as well people within the company. It is important that employees and employers do not slander each other. Speak truth in love!

10. Do not covet what others have been given by God.
    Be content and grateful for what God has blessed you with. Do not crave what God has given to others. Live life with gratitude and trust in God's provision.

The Ten Commandments always provide a clear path to excel and succeed in all areas of life. When God says to hide His Word in our hearts so we may not sin against Him, this includes the Ten Commandments. It guides

God's people to make wise decisions that definitively impact eternity.

God demonstrated His powerful presence when His chosen man, Moses, prepared to lead the people across the Red Sea. In order for His people to safely cross over, God went ahead of them and split the sea apart. God made the ground become dry for His people to escape the brutality of the Egyptians who were chasing them. That's typical of God. When God shows up, He always shows off His wonder-working power and possibilities.

> **God's commandments aren't just rules— they're the roadmap to lasting success.**

God Meets Us in the ALL IN and ALL OUT

One day, when Moses was twenty-five, he was walking alone in the wilderness. It was there that he encountered one of his most profound and life-altering moments with God. Suddenly, Moses came upon a burning bush out in the middle of nowhere. When he walked up to the bush, he noticed it wasn't burning up. He realized it was the fire of God's presence. God's voice spoke to Moses from the fire, telling him not to come any closer and to take off his sandals as he was standing on holy ground.[68]

Here, God used a supernaturally charged moment to tell Moses that He indeed did hear the cries of His people and wanted to set them free from their suffering and slavery. God wanted to bring them into a land that was beautiful, overflowing with milk and honey.

Moses argued with God about his ability and his strength to do what God wanted him to do. Moses, like many of us, believed he was inadequate for God to use because of his limitations. He had a stutter, or stammer, when he spoke. However, our God is the God over nature. He is never

> Live ALL IN and ALL OUT for God.

limited in any way to do anything, including rising from the dead, calming the storms, and walking on water. God gave Moses amazing signs and wonders to fortify Moses's obedience to the call of God on his life. God promises to do the same thing for you and me.

When God calls us to expand His Kingdom in the marketplace and lead a revival, God can and will do it! Each one of us is given the vision, the wisdom, and everything else that is needed to do what He has asked us to do in expanding His Kingdom. Just as God gave Moses everything he needed to do what God wanted and desired him to do, God will do the same for you and me. It wasn't Moses's self-effort or his talents or abilities. It was his availability. He was available to allow the power of God to prepare him to accomplish exactly what God asked him to accomplish. He was ALL IN and ALL OUT for God. I want God to do the same for me, because my heart is ALL IN and ALL OUT for God!

Ask yourself this: How would I like God to do for me what he did for Moses? Am I ALL IN and ALL OUT to do what God has called me to do?

NINE

We have this certain hope like a strong, unbreakable anchor holding our souls to God himself.

Hebrews 6:19

ETERNAL HOPE

One Martin Luther King Jr. Day, I had the privilege of spending the day with Bernice King, Dr. King's daughter. She spoke about the power of hope and how it fueled her father's courage to be able to accomplish the great things he did.

> Hope empowers us to become more than we imagined.

She reminded everyone that hope is not a wish—it's a force. Eternal hope, the kind found only in Christ, compels us to rise, rebuild, and believe beyond our limitations. Hope empowers us to become more than we ever thought possible; and to accomplish more than we ever believed we could.

In the marketplace, hope is not a luxury; it's a necessity.

Marketplace Power Source

Our faith guarantees us permanent access into this marvelous kindness that has given us a perfect relationship with God. What incredible joy bursts forth within us as we keep on celebrating our hope of experiencing God's glory!

But that's not all! Even in times of trouble we have a joyful confidence, knowing that our pressures will develop in us patient endurance. And patient endurance will refine our character, and proven character leads us back to hope. And this hope is not a disappointing fantasy, because we can now experience the endless love of God cascading into our hearts through the Holy Spirit who lives in us.[69]

For business leaders, entrepreneurs, and professionals facing shifting economies and relentless demands, hope offers more than emotional relief; it provides strategic clarity and spiritual grounding. The promises of God are not seasonal—they are enduring.[70] God's promises invite us to lead with the kind of peace that steadies the heart, strength that renews the weary, and wisdom that surpasses what the world measures as success.[71] Whether someone walks closely with Christ or is simply exploring, the invitation remains: to discover a hope anchored in the character of a God who listens, remembers, and redeems.[72] In a world where outcomes often feel uncertain, this kind of hope offers more than optimism, it offers assurance.

And while promises anchor us, prayer connects us. Even when words are spoken in quiet corners or offered years ago, the Bible reminds us that God stores the prayers of His people like incense before His throne.[73] They do

> **Our prayers do not expire—they are timeless expressions of faith, trust, and surrender.**

not expire, fade, or go unheard. In the marketplace, where timing is everything, it's comforting to know that our prayers are not bound by deadlines—they are timeless expressions of faith, trust, and surrender. Whether whispered in boardrooms or breathed between meetings, they remain before God, awaiting His perfect response.

Hope Propels Perspective

These amazing discoveries—hope and prayer—have been profoundly encouraging and transformational in both my life and business. Knowing with confidence that God is always on my side, by my side, and working inside me to fulfill His plan and purpose fills me with great expectations and unshakable hope! Every day, I ask God to up-size my hope and stretch it beyond comfort, beyond logic, beyond circumstance. Because I know this—His answers to our prayers will outlive us. They echo through generations, stirring faith long after the words were first spoken.

Hope isn't passive, it's a leadership posture. Prayer isn't reserved for quiet corners; it's a strategy Heaven honors. As you reflect on the power of hope and prayer in your own journey, consider the ripple effect hope and prayer could have in your business, your relationships, and your legacy.

Hope gives us a perspective that continues to build and add muscles to our faith. Lasting hope can never be self-generated or self-sustained. This kind of powerful, eternal hope comes only from God's promises—promises like this:

> Here's what Yahweh says to you: "I know all about the marvelous destiny I have in store for you, a future planned out in detail. My intention is not to harm you but to surround you with peace and prosperity and to give you a beautiful future, glistening with hope. When you call on me and come to me in prayer, I will listen to your every word. If you reach out to me, you will find me when you search for me with all your heart. I will not disappoint you," declares YAHWEH.[74]

Whenever I read or hear someone talk about this kind of hope that comes directly from God's committed heart for every person, I am encouraged to face the future with new boldness and fortified confidence. This directly impacts how I interact with my wife, my family, my friends, my colleagues, and everyone else who crosses my path each day. With a perspective of hope and an attitude of great expectation, we become what God calls an ambassador of hope.

Wings to Soar

God says in His operations manual, "But those who hope in the Lord will renew their strength. They will soar on wings like eagles; they will run and not grow weary, they will walk and not be faint."[75]

Businesses that operate God's way are rooted in hope—hope sourced from the One who is the author of all hope, our Heavenly Father. This kind of leadership doesn't just chase profits; it cultivates people. It raises up every employee to become a purveyor of hope, modeling God's character through daily actions and decisions.

Those who plant hope will reap outcomes like these:

- A continual renewal of their faith
- Constant strengthening of their inner scaffolding of self-confidence, rooted in God's affirmation of their worth and purpose
- Minds that are continuously refreshed and renewed
- Negative thinking into positive thinking
- Productivity elevated through peace and purpose
- Generating greater passion for shared vision and Kingdom-mindedness

Hope is a supernatural stabilizer. It confronts hypocrisy, uproots toxic patterns, and fuels restoration in teams and culture alike. When businesses adopt God's standard for how to see and speak to one another, they're not just preserving unity; they're cultivating environments where hearts heal, trust deepens, and growth multiplies.

But even with hope as the heartbeat, every thriving enterprise must also guard its internal culture—fostering environments where integrity is honored, resilience is built, and purpose remains clear. That's where stewardship systems begin to take root.

Members of a business rooted and grounded in hope call out what's right with their team members instead of dwelling on what's wrong with one another. Hope helps us clearly see the way to accomplish what Jesus taught us about the speck and the log:

REFUSE TO BE A CRITIC FULL OF BIAS TOWARD OTHERS, AND YOU WILL NOT BE JUDGED. FOR YOU'LL BE JUDGED BY THE SAME STANDARD THAT YOU'VE USED TO JUDGE OTHERS. THE MEASUREMENT YOU USE ON THEM WILL BE USED ON YOU. WHY WOULD YOU FOCUS ON THE FLAW IN SOMEONE ELSE'S LIFE AND FAIL TO NOTICE THE GLARING FLAWS OF YOUR OWN? HOW COULD YOU SAY TO YOUR FRIEND, "LET ME SHOW YOU WHERE YOU'RE WRONG," WHEN YOU'RE GUILTY OF EVEN MORE? YOU'RE BEING HYPOCRITICAL AND A HYPOCRITE!

FIRST ACKNOWLEDGE AND DEAL WITH YOUR OWN "BLIND SPOTS," AND THEN YOU'LL BE CAPABLE OF DEALING WITH THE "BLIND SPOT" OF YOUR FRIEND.[76]

These powerful words are foundational to building a hope-centered culture that operate God's way. One of today's heroes of hope is Nick Vujicic, a global speaker and entrepreneur born without limbs. Nick lives out eternal hope in every arena—from boardrooms to pulpits. His life reminds us that hope isn't just a feeling—it's a force that fuels purpose, leadership, and Kingdom impact."[77]

> If you can't get a miracle, become one.
> —Nick Vujicic

Hope is essential to trusting in God to be in control of every detail of our activities. But having hope doesn't mean that we will never fail or that we will never suffer from the hurt or pain of brokenness. Instead, hope sprouts wings to soar over troubled waters of adversity, conflict, and loss.

If you go around with critical eyes and judgmental talk you'll ruin the hope of any business seeking to please God! Hope breeds peace with profits. Whenever destructive, toxic behavior is detected, it must be ruthlessly rooted out—or it will cause emotional cancer in the business!

Champions vs. Chumps

Another great story from the Bible is about a man named Daniel. Daniel demonstrated that his outstanding job for doing business God's way got him promoted by the king himself to oversee the entire kingdom. This promotion stirred jealousy, anger, and bitterness among those who were passed over. Many administrators, supervisors, power brokers, and status seekers relentlessly conspired to find Daniel's every fault and weakness so they could remove him.

Just like in Daniel's time, too often businesses are sabotaged by the two most deadly sins: pride and greed! We are all very familiar with the notion that birds of a feather flock together. Pride and greed unite the naysayers and negative people around what they are against.

I call these naysayers and negative people—"marketplace chumps." Chumps are those who are foolish and easily deceived. They are very negative critical people who believe the lie that "everything is always about me." Any business or organization that has workers with this toxic mindset, must be ruthlessly and thoroughly rooted out before it infects others with a sense of entitlement that will destroy hope and unity.

Daniel was the opposite of a chump. He was a champ! A champ lives with the purposes of magnifying and multiplying hope. A champ has a positive attitude! A champ believes that it's not about me! The character of a champ is always winsomely hope-filled. A champ isn't chasing what they can get; rather, they run after what they can give! The champ does not desire to get more; rather, they are committed to giving more and empowering others! Every business committed to doing business God's way intentionally seeks out and cultivates champions. A champ wants to instill the heart and mind of a champ in every customer, employee, vendor, family member, owner, board member, and everyone else that crosses their paths.

Jesus is the ultimate Champ. In fact, He is the model champ! It is my deep, supreme desire to become more like Champ Jesus every day—in every way. My heart yearns to be a God-honoring champ! How about you, my friend?

When Daniel went through difficulty, challenges, and trials he stood strong for God. In fact, he ended up literally being thrown into a den of hungry lions! Are you willing to be unpopular in secular business and perhaps be thrown into the lion's den for Christ?

Here is Daniel's story of bold faith from chapter 6 in the book of Daniel:

> He [King Darius] also appointed three chief officials to watch over the work of these governors so that the king's interests might not suffer, and Daniel was one of these three. Now Daniel had an extraordinary spirit and possessed exceptional qualities. He so distinguished himself among all

the chief officials and the governors that Darius intended to set him over his entire kingdom.

For that reason, the chief officials and the governors were stirred to seek some pretext against Daniel regarding his governmental affairs. But because he was trustworthy, no one could find any error or fault in him nor could they uncover any negligence or misconduct. Finally, his accusers said to themselves, "We will never find grounds for accusation against this Daniel unless it is related to his obedience to the law of his God."

So these 122 powerful politicians consulted together as a group to entrap Daniel. And they went to speak to the king and said to him, "King Darius, live forever! All the officials of your kingdom—your high officials, administrators, advisers, and governors—we are all agreed that by royal decree the following prohibition should be enforced strictly: for thirty days, no one is to pray to any god or man except to you, O king; otherwise, he must be thrown into the lions' den. Now therefore, let the king issue this written, irrevocable decree that cannot be altered according to the unchanging law of the Medes and the Persians."

So King Darius signed the written decree.

Even after Daniel learned that the king had officially signed his decree, he continued his regular custom of praying at three set times a day. He went to the upper chamber of his house and opened the windows facing toward Jerusalem. Then he got down on his knees to pray, and he offered his grateful praise to God as he always had done.

Then all those who conspired against Daniel came and spied on him. They found him praying to God and asking him for help. So they approached the king and reminded him of his royal decree: "Your Majesty, did you not sign a decree forbidding everyone for thirty days to pray to any god or man except to you, O king, under penalty of being thrown into the lions' den?"

"Yes, I did, and my decree is final," the king answered. "It is irrevocable according to the law of the Medes and Persians."

They then told the king, "We discovered that Daniel, one of the foreign Jewish exiles, pays no heed to you, O king, and ignores the decree you have signed. For he prays to his God three times a day."

When King Darius heard this, he was deeply grieved and sought to find a way he could rescue Daniel from his fate. For most of that day until sundown, he wrestled within himself over how Daniel could be spared. But these powerful politicians went back to see the king and insisted, "Bear in mind, Your Majesty, that according to the law of the Medes and Persians, every edict or decree of the king is irrevocable."

So, the king gave orders to have Daniel brought in and cast into the lions' den. But before they threw him into the lions' den, the king said to Daniel, "Your God, whom you serve so faithfully, he will surely come to rescue you."

A large stone was then brought and placed over the opening of the den, and the king sealed it with his own signet ring and with the signet rings of each of his nobles so that Daniel's fate might not be changed. Then the king returned to his palace, where he spent the night fasting; he had no supper brought to him and could not sleep a wink.

At the first sign of dawn, the king rose from his bed and hurried off to the lions' den. As he drew near the den of lions, he called out to Daniel with a trembling voice: "O Daniel, servant of the living God, has your God, whom you serve so faithfully, been able to rescue you from the lions?"

Then he heard a voice; it was Daniel—he was still alive! "O king, live forever," answered Daniel. "My God sent his angel, who sealed the mouths of the lions. I am unharmed and without a scratch. For I have been found innocent before my God and before you, too, O king. I have committed no wrong."

The king was beside himself with joy! And he gave orders to have Daniel taken up out of the lions' den. When the servants brought him up from the den, they could find no trace of injury on his body because he had trusted in his God. Then at the king's command, those politicians who had maliciously plotted against Daniel, along with their wives and children, were arrested and flung into the lions' den. And before they reached the bottom, the lions pounced on them and devoured them, bones and all.

After that, King Darius wrote the following to all the people groups of his kingdom, those of every nation, tribe, and tongue throughout the land:

> May peace and prosperity be greatly multiplied to you!
>
> I hereby decree that throughout my royal dominion, all people everywhere will tremble in fear before the God whom Daniel worships.
>
> He is the living God, enduring forever.
>
> His kingdom will never be destroyed, and his dominion continues without end.
>
> He is a mighty savior and deliverer.
>
> He performs astonishing miracles in heaven and on earth,

He *alone* has rescued Daniel from the claws of the lions.

From then on, Daniel prospered greatly during the reign of Darius and during the reign of Cyrus the Persian.[78]

Anchored in Hope

Wow! Just as the outcomes of hope seem too good to be true, this story also seems too good to be true. But the fact is, Daniel's story is too good *not* to be true! Daniel held on wholeheartedly to hope. He knew that no matter what hap-

> It's impossible to do business God's way without hope!

pened, this God-given hope is always stronger, more able, and more than enough to sustain anyone through hopeless, or difficult times. God's hope continually sustains even the most desperate soul. It's impossible to do business God's way without hope!

Ask yourself this: What is my hope quotient? Am I willing to measure it? Am I willing to raise it?

TEN

For here is the way God loved the world—he gave his only, unique Son as a gift. So now everyone who believes in him will never perish but experience everlasting life.
John 3:16

So above all else, let love be the beautiful prize for which you run.
1 Corinthians 13:13

THE GREATEST OF ALL IS LOVE

The Bible tells the greatest love story ever written. Nothing else even comes close to the unconditional, nonjudgmental love described in its pages. Even the beloved children's song is simple and profound, "Jesus loves me this I know, for the Bible tells me so."

Not too many businesses talk about their bottom line being driven with love. Yet the greater a business operates with love, the more successful, creative, innovative, and resilient it becomes, which is far more eternally rewarding than simply financial gain. Financial success is important; nevertheless, it is always temporary. Love-filled success is always permanent and everlasting.

Jesus made the formula clear. True business success begins with two foundational commandments:

Love the Lord your God with every passion of your heart, with all the energy of your being, and with every thought that is within you." This is a great and supreme commandment. And the second is like it in importance: "You must love your friend in the same way you love yourself.[79]

The Language of Love

When I first started dating my wife, Blakney, I ended a text with the words "Love, Walt."

She later asked, "What do you mean, you love me?"

I fumbled around for words to explain, turning to ancient Greek distinctions:

- **Phileo**, the friendship kind of love
- **Eros**, the physical, sensual love
- **Agape**, the highest, most selfless love—a reflection of God's perfect heart

I acknowledge that as we courted, I began with friendship love and resolved to grow our relationship into all its expressions—ultimately pursuing the highest attainable goal: Agape. Agape loves unconditionally, nonjudgmentally. This kind of love, I believe, makes all relationships—those at home, in the community, and inside our businesses—truly permanent and eternally successful. Agape love must be woven into the very fabric, the heart and soul, of a business committed to operating God's way. Paul talks about this in 1 Corinthians 13:4-13.

AGAPE—PERFECT LOVE IN MOTION
Perfect love is patient under pressure.
Perfect love chooses kindness in every circumstance.
Perfect love gives generously, and selflessly.
Perfect love walks in humility and respect.
Perfect love believes the best and forgives the rest.
Perfect love celebrates honesty and truth.
Perfect love focuses on what is good and pure.
Perfect love is unstoppable—loyal, faithful, and forever enduring.

God's love isn't just a principle—it's the heartbeat of business done His way. Love leads the way in developing a thriving business. If we measure our bottom line by financial gain alone, we never become truly profitable. If we only measure our business success by the number of customers, we will never succeed in doing business God's way. However, if we measure our business by how much we love people, we will have a business that people love to do business with, and our customers will tell many others that our business loves people more than profit. Love for all people has a reputation that is attractive and appreciated. In other words, the business of love has present-day and eternal rewards that are more valuable than gold.

The Canopy of Love

The Bible urges, "Above all, constantly echo God's intense love for one another, for love will be a canopy over a multitude of sins."[80] No person nor any business is mistake-free or perfect. We need to have a canopy of love over our businesses to protect us from conflict and criticism, preserving unity and purpose.

This business counsel from the Bible invites us to join ourselves so closely to God that our life echoes His unconditional, nonjudgmental love toward one another. Every business committed to doing business God's way integrates operationally as well as culturally to become God's echo that consistently emulates great, passionate love for every customer, every employee, every vendor, every supervisor, every owner, and everyone else that in any way comes in contact with that business. This extravagant display of love pleases God immensely!

Recent research supports the fact: when we do what we love and love the people we serve, they will love what we do. That is flourishing. That is doing business God's way.

Love creates transformation. It turns casual customers into raving fans. When super satisfied customers become your greatest evangelists, both economically as well as spiritually, you've discovered the ultimate prize: love.

Every business seeking to ignite the flame of an Epic Marketplace Revival must become more than a transactional experience for strangers. Genuine love seeks to meaningfully transform customers into friends. It begins with a vocabulary of encouraging words, a genuine, friendly smile, and a sincere desire to meet the needs of those you serve. Love is expressed through irresistible gestures of care and concern—through listening, adapting, and showing interest in their journey.

> When we do what we love and love the people we serve, they will love what we do.

Even if you aren't able to serve people in the way they initially expected, you can still encourage—and even pray for them. You can ask God to bless and care for them and meet their needs in ways beyond your reach. If they're open to letting you, verbally witness to them how deeply God loves them.

God welcomes us to pray about anything. The outcomes and answers to our prayers are in His hands, not ours. Our job is to pray. Faith-filled prayers work wonders because God promised to answer our prayers!

Love in the Marketplace

In today's rapidly shifting landscape, artificial intelligence (AI) has captured the world's attention. From automation to algorithms, it offers efficiency and innovation—but there's one thing it can't replicate: love.

AI doesn't feel. It doesn't cherish. It lacks intrinsic values, soulfulness, and moral discernment. As impressive as it may be, AI cannot look into a human heart and offer compassion, forgiveness, or spiritual understanding.

After thousands of businesses were studied, it's been determined that 80% of America's 156,000,000 workers are unhappy at work and do not feel loved and appreciated.[81] If the average person spends over 90,000 hours of their life in the workplace feeling unloved and unhappy, then we desperately need an Epic Marketplace Revival.

Too many businesses have cultures that are built around fear and cutthroat competition. It becomes all about making more money instead of developing greater love, collaboration, and compassion. Too many of today's workers end up suffering in silence, sadness, and oftentimes burnout—not because they're incapable, but because they feel unseen and unappreciated. The human resource department, although it has a place in business and is a necessary component, is not equipped to make sure each person is cared for mentally, emotionally, physically, and spiritually.

Lead with Love

But what if every company was committed to showing love inside and outside of its building?

Every person longs to be considered as more than a resource or a commodity. People want to be deeply loved, cherished, and appreciated.

One powerful way to nurture a loving culture is by embedding care into everyday systems—integrating healing and dignity directly into operational policies and procedures. Instead of treating challenges as disruptions to be managed, businesses can choose to value each individual not as a problem to solve, but as a precious soul to support and empower. People need to know that when they're tested and fully invested, their leadership can be trusted.

> **No matter what unfolds—in business, in leadership, or in life— Love Always Wins!**

So remember: No matter what unfolds—in business, in leadership, or in life—*Love Always Wins*!

This isn't just the conclusion to a chapter. It's the heartbeat of this entire book. From stewardship to strategy, systems to seasons of struggle, every lesson, every tool, and every principle we've explored points back to this: *We were designed to lead with love.*

Love brings clarity to our calling.
Love fuels integrity in the marketplace.
Love transforms transactions into testimonies.
Love invites Heaven's wisdom into earthly work.

As you take these insights forward into your life, your team, your decisions, and your dreams—may you never forget:

You were made for this. You were made to lead with love. And when love leads, everything changes.

Ask yourself this: Am I willing to boldly go after a life and business of putting Christ's love first as if my life depended on it? Because it does.

AFTERWORD

My hope is that the message written in this book, *Epic Marketplace Revival: Doing Business God's Way*, has encouraged believers in Jesus Christ and engaged nonbelievers to invite Jesus to be the CEO of their lives.

If you have never confessed your sin and asked Jesus to forgive you of all your sins, you can repeat a simple prayer right now. Some may ask, What exactly is sin? The Greek word for *sin* is the same Greek word used for describing someone missing the mark in archery. We all have missed the mark morally and spiritually, which is why we ALL need the Savior, who is Jesus Christ.

In 1 John 1:9, we read, "But if we freely admit our sins when his light uncovers them, he will be faithful to forgive us every time. God is just to forgive us our sins because of Christ, and he will continue to cleanse us from all unrighteousness."

Do not let another minute pass in your life, now is the time to pray this simple prayer:

Jesus, I know I am a sinner.
I believe that You died on the cross for all of my sins.
Jesus, please forgive me and set me free from all of my sins.
Today, I declare that I believe in You, Jesus, as my Lord and Savior.
I choose to trust You with my whole life, including my business.
Help me to wholeheartedly follow You from this day forward.
Thank you for hearing and answering my prayer of surrendering my life, all and only to You, Jesus Christ, as my personal Lord and Savior.
Amen.

If you prayed this prayer, we would love to hear from you. Please email us at info@epicmarketplacerevival.com.

We would love to gift you a Bible to help guide you with wisdom and truth as you begin this new faith journey. We want you to grow in Love, Thanksgiving, and the Enjoyment of God as you read and receive His guidance for how to live your new life in Christ!

If your business or organization would like to order copies in multiples, please email us directly at info@marketplacerevival.com.

If you would like to schedule the authors to speak at your next business event, church, podcast, or other event, please email info@epicmarketplacerevival.com.

GETTING TO KNOW
WALT AND BLAKNEY

Dr. Walt Kallestad is a twenty-time author with major publishing houses, a guest speaker on television and radio programs, and a global trainer of pastors and leaders at conferences throughout the world.

Walt grew up as a preacher's son, where God developed his tender heart and appreciation for pastors and their families as well as the church staff and their families. His heart-tug to attend seminary and become an ordained minister did not happen until his son experienced a near death event at the age of three. After the miracle of his son's recovery, God's call became so irresistibly strong on Walt's life for full-time ministry, he could no longer ignore it. It was then that he enrolled in Luther Theological Seminary in St. Paul, Minnesota, earning his Master of Divinity. Years later he received his Doctor of Ministry from Fuller Seminary in Pasadena, California.

Walt has a saying: "If it's odd, it must be God." While Walt was at Fuller, God downloaded to him a blueprint for developing a church campus of two hundred acres. He knew only God could provide for such a feat, especially since his life's verse had always been Philippians 4:13: "I can do all things through Christ who strengthens me." (NKJV) Walt's phone alarm is set for 4:13 each day to remind him of God's promise.

Walt's first commission as a pastor was at Community Church of Joy (CCOJ) in Glendale, Arizona. It was here that God gave him a clarion call and passion to build a marketplace mission center for people who did not go to church. During Walt's time as a senior pastor at CCOJ, God did just that. It was here that the previous download of the two-hundred-acre campus was born. The church thrived and brought thousands to worship by providing healthy church ministry, a Christian school that would raise up the next generation of Christian leaders, a senior-living center, a place to live for young adults with special needs, a medical facility, a fitness center, a memorial garden, multifamily housing, and retail spaces for successful businesses as well as other discipling features. It was at CCOJ that Walt and his late wife, Mary, raised their two children.

This God-sized campus quickly became a compelling training and equipping center for more than fifty thousand pastors and leaders from around the world. When he handed the reins over to his successor nearly forty years later, Dream City Church welcomed Community Church of Joy into its family. Truly another God-sized story.

Walt's heart has always been to save lost souls for Jesus through marketplace ministry. Having spent time with Billy Graham in his career, Walt agrees with Rev. Graham's prophesy that the next great revival would take place in the marketplace. This vision is one of eternal purpose versus the world's purpose. Throughout Walt's career, and continuing today, God has always placed him with marketplace influencers and leaders to encourage and equip them so they can fulfill their God-given visions, but more importantly, so they can fulfill the Great Commission—to win lost souls to Christ.

Today, Walt continues to be involved in mentoring and motivating pastors and business leaders as well as investing his time and talents authoring and producing books, podcasts, and curriculum to raise up marketplace leaders with the skills and tools to live and lead God's way!

In November 2022, Walt married Blakney Boggs Kallestad who is an amazing godly woman, a successful civil litigator, and a retired PGA/LPGA golf teaching professional. Together they are *ALL IN*. Their hearts are aligned in chasing after God's heart and the lost through marketplace ministry. They are working together to equip and raise up a new generation of leaders who are *ALL IN* and seeking to do life God's way.

Walt enjoys worshiping with his wife, daily devotions, writing, traveling, golfing, daily ocean walks, and Mickey Mouse.

Blakney Kallestad grew up in Dallas, Texas, with a rich family legacy of faith and ministry. Her grandfather was a lay minister, her father an early supporter of World Vision, and her cousin Frank Boggs the first vocal artist with Word Records. It is not surprising that her current life chapter included becoming a minister's wife when she married Walt Kallestad.

Her life's tapestry has had many twists and turns throughout, but it has become the most beautifully woven masterpiece, where God has kept His promise of Romans 8:28: "So we are convinced that every detail of our lives is continually woven together for good, for we are his lovers who have been called to fulfill his designed purpose."

Her faith journey began at eight years old when she accepted Jesus and was baptized by W. A. Criswell at First Baptist Dallas. Active in the church, she could always be found singing in the choir or at church camp in the summertime. Also, around eight years old, she began her love affair with golf and aspired to become professional. She was competitive in the sport and garnered the Dallas City Champion state ranking and invitations to play internationally.

At the tender age of seventeen, she moved to California and played golf for the University of Southern California while studying prelaw. However, it would be years later before she pursued her call to become a lawyer. After graduating from USC with a theater degree, she became an PGA/LPGA Class A teaching professional and ran a film production company. Even after she became a lawyer she continued to teach for many years. She retired after twenty-five years of teaching golf.

At age thirty-nine, after a series of life-shattering events, she heard God clearly say, "It is time, time to pursue the dream of becoming a lawyer." God continued to open doors, and through an amazing series of events, she went to Liberty University School of Law on scholarship and received her J.D. in 2008. In 2009, Blakney was admitted to the California Bar, and in 2018, the United States Supreme Court. Today she is a successful civil trial attorney.

Throughout her life, she has always known there is an enormous call on her life, one that is about more than professional careers or making money. Although she sought God's call on her life and tried to hear His voice, at times she pursued the wrong things. At a crossroads with her career in April 2022, she gave God her all and told Him she was "ALL IN." Shortly thereafter, God introduced her to her husband, Walt Kallestad, which if you ask either of them, they will tell you it is a "God-tale, and not a fairytale."

As a natural born trainer and great communicator, Blakney's desire is to use all the talents and skills God has blessed her with to encourage marketplace leaders and influencers to do life God's way in all areas of their lives, including family, relationships, and work.

She and her husband enjoy worshipping together, traveling, USC football, watching wholesome movies, and walking at the ocean.

NOTES

Preface

[1] Genesis 32:22–32.

Introduction

[2] Psalm 119.

Chapter 1: Why Is My Father's Business My Most Important Business?

[3] 2 Corinthians 5:1

[4] David Greene, *Leadership Not by the Book, 12 Unconventional Principles to Drive Incredible Results* (Baker Books, 2022), 13–16.

[5] Isaiah 40:8.

[6] John 11:25–26.

[7] Community Church of Joy, Glendale, Arizona. Later, this Glendale campus became part of Dream City Church's multiple campuses based out of Phoenix, Arizona.

[8] Acts 16:31.

[9] Luke 18:18–30.

[10] The Greek word for "disciple" is *mathētēs*, which means learner or pupil.

[11] Matthew 16:24–27.

[12] Proverbs 16:23.

[13] Philippians 2:1–5.

[14] 1 Corinthians 13:4–8a.

[15] Luke 6:38.

[16] Proverbs 11:24.

[17] Proverbs 11:25.

[18] Proverbs 11:30.

[19] Mark 3:24.

Chapter 2: Keep Sharply Focused on Saving One Soul at a Time

[20] 2 Corinthians 5:17–18a.

[21] Mark 2:21–22.

[22] 1 Samuel 15:22 (NLT).

[23] 1 Corinthians 9:24–27.

[24] Philippians 1:21 (NKJV).

[25] Philippians 3:8.

[26] Matthew 6:19–20 (NKJV).

Chapter 3: Choose Your Inner Circle Wisely!

[27] Matthew 6:33.

[28] Psalm 1:2.

[29] Philippians 2:12–13.

[30] Philippians 2:16.

[31] Proverbs 3:6.

[32] Proverbs 3:7.

[33] Proverbs 3:9–10.

[34] Matthew 22:37.

[35] Matthew 22:39.

Chapter 4: Grow a Silver-Dollar Attitude and an Eternally Focused Heart and Mind

[36] Tim Keller, *Generous Justice: How God's Grace Makes Us Just* (Dutton, 2010), 60.

[37] 2 Corinthians 9:7–8 (NLT).

[38] Proverbs 11:25.

[39] If anyone has not accepted Christ as their Savior, please go to the afterword in this book to be guided in a prayer of salvation. If you do this, we would love to hear from you and encourage you on your next steps.

[40] Matthew 6:13b (NKJV).

[41] Colossians 2:2–3 (NIV).

[42] Ephesians 2:10.

[43] John 9:4.

[44] Luke 19:5.

[45] Luke 19:10.

[46] Luke 19:8b.

Chapter 5: Make a Great Commitment to God's Great Commandment and God's Great Commission

[47] Matthew 22:37–39.

[48] Matthew 28:18b–20.

[49] 1 Corinthians 2:9 (NLT).

Chapter 6: How to Build a Rock-Solid Business That Can Last Forever!

[50] Matthew 7:24-27.

[51] John 15:4–8.

[52] Romans 12:3.

[53] Ephesians 5:2b.

[54] Proverbs 12:17, 19, 22.

[55] 2 Peter 1:3–11.

[56] 2 Peter 1:10-11.

[57] Proverbs 18:21.

[58] Matthew 15:10–12.

[59] Matthew 15:13–14.

[60] Matthew 15:17–20a.

Chapter 7: Businesses That Are Built to Last Excel at Exceptional Hospitality

[61] Luke 10:30–37.

[62] Luke 10:38-42.

[63] Matthew 25:31–40.

[64] John 13:3–17.

Chapter 8: The Everlasting Power of Bold Faith

[65] Matthew 17:20 (NIV).

[66] Galatians 6:9 (NIV).

[67] Matthew 5:21–22.

[68] Exodus 3:5 (NIV).

Chapter 9: Eternal Hope

[69] Romans 5:2–5.

[70] Psalm 145:13.

[71] Philippians 4:6–7.

[72] Psalm 145:18–19.

[73] Revelation 5:8.

[74] Jeremiah 29:11–14a.

[75] Isaiah 40:31 (NIV).

[76] Matthew 7:1–5.

[77] Nick Vujicic, *Life Without Limits: Inspiration for a Ridiculously Good Life* (New York: Doubleday Religion, 2010), 17.

[78] Daniel 6:2–28.

Chapter 10: The Greatest of All Is Love

[79] Matthew 22:37–39.

[80] 1 Peter 4:8.

[81] Gallup. *State of the Global Workplace: 2024 Report.* Washington, D.C.; Gallup, Inc., 2024. https://healthyworkcompany.com/wp-content/uploads/2024/08/state-of-the-global-workplace-2024-key-insights.pdf.

www.ingramcontent.com/pod-product-compliance
Lightning Source LLC
Chambersburg PA
CBHW061756120626

46550CB00005B/2019